THE POPE AND ITALY

His Holiness, Pope Pius XI.

The Pope and Italy

By
WILFRID PARSONS, S.J.
Editor of "America"

THE AMERICA PRESS
1929

To

P. J. P.
and
A. C. P.

FILIAL HOMAGE

CONTENTS

———

The Roman Question Is Settled

WITH almost startling suddenness, considering the long years that it had dragged out, the old Roman Question was settled. It is a great triumph for the present Holy Father, and his children the world over will unite in loving congratulations to him. He has brought religious peace to Italy, and best of all, peace with honor. Not a principle has been sacrificed, and yet the civic ideal of a united Italy has not been touched, but rather enhanced. Italians can at last feel secure in giving allegiance to their State without the guilty feeling of doing violence to the Church which that State had grievously wronged.

Honor is due to those who worked obscurely and hopefully to this end for so long, but most of all to Signor Mussolini for his determination to see it through, and to Pope Pius XI for the striking spirit of conciliation with which he met the crisis.

For the settlement did not come without great sacrifices on the part of the Holy See. It has renounced at last all the legal claims it rightfully possessed to the city of Rome and to the old Papal States, and on its part the Italian State has in turn acknowledged the sovereign independence of the Holy See. The territory which the Papacy can claim as that in which it is supreme in sovereignty is not much greater than that in which it has carried on since 1870; yet it does not hold this territory as a gift of the Italian State, but by its own right. This right united Italy has at last recognized.

The history of the great "Question" is fairly well known. When Rome was usurped by the Piedmontese King on September 20, 1870, the Pope retired to the Vatican and uttered his first protest to the world. The Italian Parliament made a half-hearted attempt to settle the Pope's status by the "Law of Guarantees" in 1871. The effect of this law was merely to place the Pope in the position of a private Italian citizen in his episcopal city, somewhat like that of the Archbishop of Canterbury at Lambeth; under it the Papal independence would not have been much greater than that of the English Primate in the national Established Church of England.

The Popes had to reject the Law of Guarantees, but since to go out from the Vatican in such a situation would have been tantamount to setting up as national a religious status which by its nature must be supra-national, as we shall see, the Popes have ever since been prisoners in the Vatican, prisoners by legal necessity though not by physical violence. As the years passed on, protest was renewed, but Italy was in the grip of a Masonic clique and no real hope was ever entertained of a solution. This grip was broken by Mussolini and his Fascists, and the time was at last ripe for a settlement. On its part the Vatican had little by little recognized that there was no hope of recovering its lost provinces and cities.

It is necessary to recall the principles which underly this historic question and its no less historic solution. The Catholic Church is by Divine law a "perfect society" of men, that is, one deriving its rights from no man or group of men, from no State or international law. Moreover, it is by the terms of its foundation a universal society; it is not a national Church, but the Catholic Church. If it were a mere national institution, like the Anglican establishment, its head could afford to live like a private citizen in the capital of his own nation.

But to the Pope Englishmen and Indians, Frenchmen and Patagonians, Germans and Chinese, Italians and Zulus, Spaniards and Eskimos, Irishmen and Egyptians, Americans and Armenians, all owe a like spiritual allegiance. He is the spiritual Father of them all. It is, then, of the most supreme necessity that he be not the subject of any prince or Parliament, but independent and sovereign in his own right. The merest suspicion that he is the catspaw of any national Government in anything that he does or says in his spiritual apostolate would be fatal to his influence.

We who have seen the attempts made during our recent Presidential election to make him out a "foreigner," that is, a man with sinister designs

on our own civil sovereignty, have reason to acknowledge the justice of this position. He must be
a citizen of no nation, but placed above and apart
from the nations. Only then can he exercise his
God-given prerogative of Vice-Gerent of Christ.

The problem of all these years has been how to
establish this unique but necessary position, in the
face of the rightful demands of Italians to their
national unity. In all the years before 1870, when
the Italian peninsula was a mere peninsula, but not
a nation, a mere group of small States, but not a
European Power, the situation was different.
Territory, possessed by sovereign right, has always
been recognized before international law as the
sole guarantee of independence. That territory
and that independence the Popes then possessed.

With the fall of Rome, the Question took shape.
Rome was the Popes' by immemorial right; it was
also the natural and predestined capital of the new
Italian State. The ensuing deadlock lasted until
on the one side the hard reality of the definite loss
had been fully realized, and, on the other, there
was found a Government not animated by a desire

to trick and bargain, but one in whom the Pope could have a natural confidence. This he has no doubt felt that he has found at last, and Catholics the world over can but rejoice at the happy conclusion.

The documents signed by Cardinal Gasparri and Signor Mussolini at the Lateran Palace on February 11, 1929, and a day later on the seventh anniversary of Pope Pius' coronation solemnly celebrated in St. Peter's, were essentially two, for there were two questions to settle, not one.

There was the *Roman* Question, the question of the Pope's independent status, and there was the *Italian* Question, the question of the regulation of the relations between Church and State in Italy. The Italian Question, it has always been held by the Popes, could not be settled until the Roman Question was settled. It is true that similar agreements have been made between the Holy See and France, Lithuania, Rumania, Chile, Argentina, and other countries, by those treaties which in the Church's case are known as Concordats. But with Italy there was no settlement until justice had been done by it to the Holy See, by a restoration of the occupied territory, or at least by a formal recognition of the Church's sovereignty in a territory, however small. This it has at last done, and the Roman Question is settled.

But as we set out to give an explanation of the recent act by which the Question was settled, we are confronted by several difficulties which have to be faced.

The modern world, careless of history and not over-solicitous of pure logic, finds it hard to see why there should have been any Question at all. Was it not merely a matter of insistence by the Popes on an imaginary right which existed only in their own desire for power? Have we not progressed to a point where separation of Church and State, of the spiritual and the temporal powers, is almost a dogma of political thought? How then can we countenance such a reactionary step as to set up once more the Pope as King? Why, also, should the Catholic Church, any more than any other religious body, claim the position of a sovereign State?

The answer to all these questions, and others like them, is that the Temporal Power of the Pope was historically inevitable and is logically necessary. Let us take up these ideas in order.

Temporal Sovereignty Was Historically Inevitable

THE first step in any study of the matter is to turn the pages of history. What we find there is the *fact* that the Popes did have temporal power, did rule by right over territory, and that the nations of the world did unanimously recognize their independent sovereignty in that territory from the years 800 to 1870. No theorizing about the Papacy can conjure that fact away.

How did that fact come to pass?

The legal basis of the right of the Christian Church, as such, one in fact and theory, to hold property was recognized anew by Constantine in the Edict of Milan in 321 A. D.[1] It is probable that to that law the Emperor added an actual gift,

[1]The Church's right to buy, sell and hold property in the form of *collegia* had already been recognized by the pagan Emperors. Cf. H. Thurston, S.J., Property, Ecclesiastical, Catholic Encyclopedia, Vol. XII, p. 466ff. The legal rite to inherit by will was added by the Edict. For the text of the Edict, see Mourret, Histoire Générale de l'Eglise, I, 509.

which was the Lateran Palace,[2] in which by a striking turn of history, the latest Pope irrevocably signed away his right to the city of Rome.

From that time the Holy See added to its possessions by donation of large estates, until it owned immense possessions in Italy, Africa, Gaul, Dalmatia and the Orient.[3] The incomes from these landed estates, called the "Patrimony of St. Peter," were used for all the multiform social, educational and religious enterprises which the destiny and spiritual vocation of the Popes led them to undertake in a world that was falling into pieces and in which it was the only stable thing.[4] These donations ceased about 600 A. D. It is important to note, however, that the Pope was not yet the Sovereign of these lands; royal title in them was still

[2]Or more probably it was the Empress Fausta who gave this property. It is generally agreed that Constantine made many gifts to Pope St. Silvester. Cf. Mann, The Lives of the Popes in the Middle Ages, Vol. I, Part 2, p. 282.

[3]On the origin and growth of the "Patrimony of St. Peter" see Grisar, History of Rome and the Popes in the Middle Ages, II, pp. 40 and 82-3; Mann, loc. cit.; and Gosselin, The Power of the Pope, (Trans., London, 1853), I, pp. 96 and 179.

[4]Grisar, loc. cit.

held by the Roman Empire, in its seat at Byzantium, or Constantinople.[5]

The terrible struggle between Byzantium, which felt the West slipping from its fingers, and the nearest of the Germanic tribes, the Lombards, began in 568. In the ensuing chaos, the Popes, as the largest and most powerful of all the land-owners of the Italian peninsula were naturally looked up to as the protectors of the other and smaller nobles.[6] Pope Stephen II, having made one last vain appeal to the Bosphorus, bethought himself of crossing the Alps and winning the Franks.

It was a historic step, and it entitles this Pope to be called the Father of the Temporal Power. At Quiercy, or Kiersy, Pepin promised in 754 to make him sovereign of the Duchy of Rome, the Exarchate of Ravenna, the Marches of Ancona, and the strip of land between.[7] In 756, he redeemed the promise on the spot. In 774, Pepin's son, Charlemagne, was called on by Pope Adrian

[5]Mourret, op. cit., III, p. 300, note 2.
[6]Grisar, op. cit., II, p. 39ff. Mann, op. cit., p. 287.
[7]Mann, op. cit., p. 300.

I to renew the promise and in 781 he definitely established the Pope on his throne by force of arms.

Legally, the sovereign of these lands, the Emperor at Byzantium, no longer able to exercise his sovereign rights through the Exarchate at Ravenna or to protect his subjects against the Lombards, had forfeited these rights; they had been taken by right of conquest by Pepin and formally bestowed by him upon the Pope.[8] With expansions and contractions these territories remained the Pope's in fact until 1870, and in right until he himself signed nearly all of them away in 1929. The right of sovereignty which they implied was never abdicated, and Italy formally recognized it in 1929, with the natural result of recognition by the Pope of the unification of Italy.

Now when Pope Stephen II crossed the Alps to the court of Pepin, he seems to have had two

[8]The promise and donation of Pepin are well discussed by Gosselin, op. cit., pp. 217-230. On the Pope's freedom from the Emperor at Byzantium, see ibid., p. 228; and on his not owing suzerainty to Pepin, Charlemagne and their successors, ibid., p. 255. The original texts of the Papal agreements with Pepin are lost; the *Liber Pontificalis* is the source for the facts. Duchesne, The Beginnings of the Temporal Sovereignty of the Popes, p. 36.

things in mind. He went as spokesman for the peoples of the Italian peninsula, to find a new protector against the Lombard enemy who was bent on subjugating them, and a protector sufficiently far away not to be suspected of wishing to settle down in their place as a new oppressor.[9]

But he had a far deeper idea than that. His journey was, in a sense, no sudden impulse; it had, in a sense, been meditated for two hundred years. In fact, ever since Constantine had providentially recognized the Christian Church, and had retired from Rome to build New Rome on the shores of the Bosphorus, this step had been taking shape.[10]

The incursion of barbarians had hastened the

[9]Duchesne, op. cit., p. 273: "The temporal power had its origin in the repugnance of the Romans to becoming Lombards, and in their inability to organize their autonomy unless the Pope was placed at its head."

[10]The Popes had exercised a *de facto* sovereignty over Rome for many years. From the time of Constantine they in common with all Bishops had many civil prerogatives. Mann; op. cit., p. 283. According to Bryce, The Holy Roman Empire, p. 95, Rome had ceased to be the political capital of the West in 476, and the Popes took over civil power in the City in increasing measure. See also Mann, op. cit., p. 288; Duchesne, op. cit., pp. 14-18. When the Byzantine Emperors left them to their fate, the last step in independence was completed. The relations with the new defenders of the Church were taken up on an entirely new basis.

decision. The leadership of Rome fell to the Bishop of Rome by default. In the logic of events, it had gradually become clearer, as great world movements do, that the Papacy, whose mission was spiritual, and with the title of custodian of civilization which inevitably devolved on it, was destined, under penalty of failing humanly, to have a place before the eyes of men and kings which should be forever inviolable. Supreme spiritual power that it was, and recognized as such by all, it should yet in a world of worldly men enjoy the only prerogative which they could respect, independent sovereignty.

Everything that happened in four centuries made this practical necessity clearer. The last straw was the demonstration that the Church's providential protector, the old Roman Empire in the West, was finally dead. Europe was henceforth doomed to national and tribal strifes. Religion was exposed to extinction. The Papacy inevitably stood temporally high above and apart from the warring factions. This was the result of its struggle to defend its prerogative of spiritual supremacy. Thus a modern writer sums it up:

One of two things had to be. Rome and the surrounding provinces had to belong either to the Pope or to another power. They could not remain *res nullius* (no man's land). But if the Pope had not possessed them, who would have been their master? A Byzantine Emperor? A Lombard King? A Frankish King? The Church and Peter, given the customs of those times, would have been condemned either to revolt or to submission. It would have meant handing over Peter to the eventual menace of a new Nero. A Pope in Rome at a time of medieval barbarity, with an emperor or king in the same town, or even a simple tribune of the people, would have made Peter the servant of Cæsar, which would have been the very negation of Peter's mission. Constantine understood this so well that after his conversion he judged it well to withdraw from Rome and transfer the seat of the Empire elsewhere.[11]

Temporal Power was historically inevitable.[12]

[11]Carrère, The Pope, p. 74. Cf. Mann, op. cit., pp. 281-282.

[12]For a long time in the nineteenth century it was the fashion of anti-clerical writers, following the Gallican prejudice of the seventeenth, to ascribe the Temporal Power to a forgery. The so-called Donation of Constantine, on which the Popes were said to lay their claim to the title of temporal sovereigns, was certainly a forgery. Gosselin, op. cit., I, p. 181. Nobody has ever been able to prove, however, that any Pope claimed temporal power previous to Stephen II on that basis, nor that any Pope subsequent to him, though many referred to it under the belief that it was genuine, made the basis of temporal power any other juridical fact than the Donation of Pepin. Cf. Gosselin, loc. cit., and Clarke, The False Decretals (Catholic Truth Society). Also Catholic Encyclopedia, Vol. V, s. v. False Decretals. All non-Catholic historians now agree on the small part the False Decretals played in the growth of Papal power. Mann, op. cit., pp. 467-472.

Temporal Sovereignty Is a Logical Necessity

EVEN, however, had events not shaped themselves as they actually did, but in some other pattern, it was certain that the Papacy, being what it was, should enjoy temporal power.

It was the necessity of logic.

It is hard for the modern world to understand this fact. We have been so long accustomed to the division of Christendom that we run the risk of regarding this condition as the natural one, and the other, that of a united Christendom, as an anomaly. We have so long entertained the idea of the equality of the divided churches before the law, that we risk forgetting that there is one Church from which all the other churches have been broken off at definite dates by scission or diminution of doctrine, and which as a historical fact derives its own existence in an unbroken line from the Apostles and the Saviour.

To understand the next step we must, therefore, divest our minds of analogies and comparisons; for there is one Church to which there is as a fact no analogy on earth, not only in its claims but in its very nature, however dimly the world recognizes this fact.

That is the Catholic Church, whose head is the successor of St. Peter in the office of Bishop of Rome.

The undoubted characteristic of this Church is its universal unity, in time and in place, historically as well as geographically: it is one with itself in a past which sprouts from the Apostles themselves, and it is one with itself in every part of the world. This fact is clearly recognized by Bryce in his "Holy Roman Empire":

The whole fabric of medieval Christianity rested upon the idea of the Visible Church. Such a Church could be in nowise local or limited. To acquiesce in the idea of National Churches would have appeared to those men, *as it must always appear when scrutinized,* contradictory to the nature of a religious body, opposed to the genius of Christianity, defensible when capable of defense at all, only as a temporary resource in the face of insuperable difficulties.[13]

[13]Bryce, Holy Roman Empire, p. 91.

No other Church has this characteristic of visible universality.

Being alone universal, therefore, it has a position in regard to the various nations of the world possessed by no other church. It is international, in the sense that its members, necessarily and also as a fact, belong to every nation. It is supranational, in the sense that in its central government it must, having members among all nations, be subject to the government of no one among the nations. If it were so subject, it would incur the penalty of losing at the same time its essential characteristic of universality and the allegiance of a large number of its members. This is true of all times; it becomes clear in such times of stress as the War of 1914-1918.

This, then, is the first logical necessity of the Catholic Church in regard to the nations of the world. As a universal spiritual power, it must be independent of any circumscribed temporal power, or forfeit its universality and risk the loss of its spiritual influence.

One of the historical documents on this aspect

of the question is the letter of Leo XIII to Cardinal Rampolla on June 15, 1887. I quote this relevant passage:

The authority of the Supreme Pontiff, instituted by Jesus Christ and conferred upon St. Peter, and through him to Us his legitimate successors, the Roman Pontiffs, is destined to perpetuate in the world to its very end the redemptive work of the Son of God. This power has been enriched by the most noble prerogatives, endowed with exalted powers of its own and juridical powers as well, such as are required in the government of a true and perfect society. Hence that authority, by its very nature and by the express will of the Divine Founder of the Church, cannot be subject to any earthly power whatever, but must actually enjoy the most ample liberty in order to carry on its sacred ministry.

For since the well-being of the entire Church depends upon this supreme power and upon the free exercise thereof, it was of the greatest importance that its original liberty and independence should be assured, guaranteed and defended throughout the ages in the person of him in whom it was invested.

. . . It must be carefully borne in mind, however, that the reason for the liberty and independence of the Papacy in the exercise of its Apostolic ministry has a greater value and a peculiarly distinctive force when applied to Rome, the natural residence of the Supreme Pontiffs, the center of the life of the Church and the capital of the Catholic world.

In Rome, where the Pontiff ordinarily resides, the center

whence he directs, teaches, and commands; so that all the
Faithful may pay him dutiful respect from every part of the
world and render him obedience with security and trust;—
it is in Rome that it is especially necessary that he be in
such status of independence that not only shall his liberty
be not in the least curtailed by anyone, but that none be
there to violate it.[14]

The Established Church of England is the
staple example of what would happen to it, if it
were not civilly independent of the Government of
the State in whose confines its Head resides. It
would become the established Church of Italy, and
suffer the loss of its universal existence.

There must, however, exist a guarantee of this
independence. Such might be the guarantee possessed by the great States of the world, an army
and navy so strong that none except a combination
of States stronger than itself would dare to violate
its independence. Or it might be the guarantee of
independence possessed by a smaller State like
Belgium. That is neutrality. This neutrality in
turn might be founded in an international agreement among the greater nations to preserve it by

[14]Acta Leonis XIII (Bruges, 1887), Vol. II, p. 280.

force of arms, or in the mere fact of a juridical status in international law, but based on no international promise of protection against aggression.[15]

This latter status is the very minimum guarantee of independence. It is, in fact, the common substratum of the other two. It is called by the technical name of sovereignty.[16] It implies two things: the right to exercise the usual civic functions in regard to its subjects, and the right of inviolability by any other body possessing sovereignty. In the light of international law as it actually exists there is no other guarantee of independence than sovereignty and all that it implies.

Once granted that a universal spiritual power like the Catholic Church needs independence in order to retain its existence and carry out its religious mission, the second logical necessity of the

[15]John Bassett Moore, Digest of International Law, I, p. 20. Belgium is given as an example for the second kind of guarantee, and Switzerland for the third.

[16]Moore, op. cit., I, p. 18: "A State is sovereign, from the point of view of the law of nations, when it is independent of every other State in the exercise of its international rights externally, and in the manner in which it lives and governs itself internally."

situation is that its Head possess sovereignty, as its only guarantee of existence.

Naked sovereignty, however, is a name without a habitation, a wraith without substance. It already implies some subjects, as we saw, and sovereignty tied to no place would be an idea, perhaps, but it would not be actual sovereignty.[17] Consequently a third element enters in, that of territory. Territory is the instrument of sovereignty in act; without it, there is sovereignty in theory, but it would not be actual, and as such, would demand no inviolability from other sovereignties. To possess sovereignty in fact, it must be *seen;* territory is the instrument of its being seen. Without territory, at least some small one, there would be no real sovereignty, except perhaps in theory, but certainly not in fact.

Here is the third logical necessity of the Church's situation: its head government, being universal by nature and spiritual by vocation, must be independent of any civil sovereignty. But in order to be so, it must possess a civil sovereignty of

[17]Moore, op. cit., p. 16.

its own, setting it apart; and civil sovereignty in fact demands that it be tied to some territory, so that all the world can see it and respect it.

This principle was very clearly set forth by Count dalla Torre, editor of the *Osservatore Romano*:

Liberty and independence, in the full meaning of the words, required by the nature of things and essential to a spiritual power, can only become concrete through the medium of sovereignty. In the present position of the law of nations such sovereignty can only exist if it is based on territory. Such principles, speaking objectively, have developed in all schools of positive law, and are accepted and admitted by the international system.[18]

The Pope must pertain to some particular State or have a State of his own. There is no middle condition possible. Grant the one and you deny the other. This is what we mean by the "Temporal Power of the Popes"; it is wholly spiritual in aim, and necessarily temporal in execution.

We shall now see how the Popes lost the Temporal Power, without incurring the loss of sovereignty, paradoxical as that might seem.

[18]Carrère, op. cit., p. 230.

The Temporal Power Is Lost

THE loss of the Temporal Power of the Popes, seen in retrospect, must also be pronounced to have been one of those inevitable movements of history which no one human agency could have prevented, for the combination of forces which actually came into play would have proved too great to resist. The often inscrutable Providence of God has more than once decreed events which human wisdom would pronounce disasters.

At the end of the Napoleonic Era, when Europe once more settled down to peace, the Italians found their country mostly in the hands of foreigners. In the North, Lombardy and Venice were a part of Austria, and Parma and Piacenza were held by the Bourbons; in the South, Naples and Sicily were likewise ruled by Bourbon princes, while other portions were under families of Austria or Lorraine. The Papal dominions, in the center,

Pius IX.

comprised about 17,218 square miles. It was inevitable, in such a state of affairs, that a movement of deliverance and unification should get under way sooner or later.

This movement, when it came, had a twofold impulse. There was a Masonic, so-called democratic, agitation, which was republican in aim and had the Carbonari and Garibaldi as its instruments;[19] and there were the dynastic ambitions of the House of Savoy, Kings of Sardinia and Piedmont.

As long as France and Austria were friends, this twofold movement had no hopes of success, but the time came when they fell out, and that was the opportunity of the insurgents. Little by little the foreigner in North and South was expelled, and then the ring closed in upon the Pope. A furious agitation against the Church raged in Italy and abroad; religious, political, dynastic, national, and personal loves and hates were inextricably mingled. Men's minds and consciences were cruelly divided. It seemed that the Italian people had as much right

[19]Reuben Parsons, Studies in Church History, VI, pp. 480-504.

to unify their country as any other, but—there was
the Pope, and they were Catholics. It is too true
that anti-religious hate animated many of the
Pope's enemies, but not all of them, nor even, it
would seem, most of them.[20]

It was thought for a time that the Pope, Pius
IX, could be persuaded to accept the post of head
of an Italian Confederation, but he would have
none of it. His claim was spiritual, not political.
His aim was independence, not dominance. His
mission was to convert the world and save it, not
to rule a world Power at the head of a cabinet.
That the proposal was made, shows how little people understood his real contention. He tried to
stem the rising tide of so-called domocratic ideas
by introducing various political "reforms" in Rome,
but in vain. The movement to unify Italy was
irresistible; an unbreakable love and an inex-
tinguishable hate joined forces to compel it. In
our country and in England the Pope had little
sympathy, for in these democratic lands men were
rather drawn to the insurgents, who called things

[20]Cf. Carrère, op. cit., pp. 191-2; 196.

by the same names which we use, though the ideas were, and have always been, poles apart.

The end came when France, in the throes of the Franco-Prussian War, had to withdraw her defending troops from Rome.[21]   On September 20, 1870, a breach was made in the Roman walls near the Porta Pia, a formal show of resistance was made by the Papal troops—mostly volunteers from France—Rome was occupied by the King, and Italian unity was achieved, in fact if not by right. The Papacy had weathered a score of frightful storms from every quarter; waves of barbarian hordes, and of armies from Spain, France and Germany, had dashed over its walls and each time had receded, leaving it in undiminished independence. It fell at last before the Italian people, leaving Rome the object of two apparently unassailable but contradictory rights: the right of United Italy to its own capital, and the immemorial right of the

[21]Some Catholic historians have accused Napoleon III of deliberate treachery in this decisive act, since the few troops withdrawn were not really needed on the front. Cf. Parsons, op. cit., VI, p. 547. It is at least probable that by it he sought to win Italian sympathy for himself.

Papacy to its own possession, which had come to it as an historical inevitability and a logical necessity.[22]

[22]It is not intended to justify the right of Italy to Rome by the so-called plebiscite of October 2, 1870, which was to signify the will of Rome but which only disgraced the new Italian Government. It is now admitted that this was a fraud. The Roman people did not vote at all; hirelings voted many times; the count was not reliable. Guggenberger, General History of the Christian Era, III, p. 340.

The Roman Question Arises

THUS arose the Roman Question. It was at its very bottom a conflict of principles, not a squabble for land. This is well put by Carrère, a French writer, in his interesting work, "The Pope."

What answer must we give to the two questions already asked: Was Italy right? Was the Papacy right? To both these questions the only answer is, yes.

I. Yes, Italy, a very ancient people going back more than a thousand years before Christianity, having in the nineteenth century once regained consciousness of her real nationality and fundamental unity, had a right to try to reunite under the control of a single Government all the regions forming that living entity which is called a nation, and consequently could not renounce Rome, that essential city, the very center of her territory and history.

II. Yes, the Papacy whose historical role has been visible and uninterrupted for nineteen centuries, and which for eleven centuries has exercised power in Rome and its neighboring territory for the greater good of the governed populaton, and with the unanimous consent of all European nations; the Papacy to which Rome was assigned by its founder; and which could never separate from it, had the right to claim this domain which it considered indispensable to its dependants and to the free exercise of its spiritual power.

The conflict of these two rights, both equally irrefutable, constitutes, properly speaking, the *Roman Question*.

It is precisely because they are both irrefutable that this question has been so burning and so ceaselessly renewed. For if one of the two rights invoked by the two parties could have been denied, diminished, or even disputed, sooner or later one of the two theories would have ousted the other.[23]

On the one side, then, there was the absolute spiritual necessity for the Papacy to be the territorial subject of no earthly power, and the consequent necessity that it exist on a territory belonging to no State; on the other side, there was the natural desire of the Italians to make Rome the capital of their new State and a certain logic in the choice of that city for this purpose.

On the one side, there was the inseparable link of the Pope to Rome, as his episcopal city; on the other, there was the reluctance of the Italians to choose another capital, for Rome is central and the traditional head of Italy. It was impossible for either to depart, yet it seemed that both could not remain as friends.

[23]Carrère, op. cit., pp. 194-5.

This tragic situation was well seen by the non-Catholic Ernest Lavisse. He writes:

Since Charlemagne deposited on the tomb of St. Peter the "title of donation," eleven centuries have rolled by. But eleven centuries do not count in the immutability of the Church . . . Italy has become a world Power. But she is not entirely at home as are the other nations. Between the Alps and the capes of Sicily the soil is not all Italian; at the center there is a palace surrounded by a garden. It is the domain of St. Peter. Here the King of Italy entereth not. . . . And in the meantime the Apostle does not cease to protest and to lament. The plaint of the immortal old man sounds like a never-stopping funeral bell tolling over the capital, Rome. Its sound disquiets and irritates kings and ministers. What is the use of being at Rome, if there is still at Rome a Roman Question?[24]

It is not surprising that until the recent very simple solution it was thought by most people that the Question was insoluble.

An attempt was, indeed, made to solve the Question soon after it arose. Spurred by worldwide condemnation of their course, and by the moderates in their own ranks, who suffered from an acute conflict of conscience, the triumphant party passed the so-called Law of Guarantees, on May 13, 1871.

[24]Quoted by Mourret, op. cit., p. 302.

This law has been freely admitted by ecclesiastical authorities to have been a masterpiece of legislation. Its terms were in striking contrast to the restrictive and intolerant terms of the national Constitution, though it is rarely remembered that this latter document (Art. I) made the Catholic the official State religion of Italy. By the Law of Guarantees, the sacredness of the person of the Sovereign Pontiff was safeguarded; royal honors were to be accorded him in all of Italy; the Vatican property was declared extra-territorial; he was allowed unhindered access to the outer world and his relations with it were to be facilitated; and an annuity of 3,225,000 lire ($622,425) was settled on him for expenses. The law was in many ways extremely wise, even generous,[25] though it allowed much previous oppressive anti-clerical legislation to remain on the statute books.

Yet Pope Pius IX refused it, and every Pope since him has continued to do so. Pius IX did so two days after it was passed, in the Encyclical of May 15, 1871. His first protest was in the En-

[25]See its text, Carrère, The Pope, pp. 250-255.

cyclical of November 1, 1870. Leo XIII lost no
time after his election, but protested on April 21,
1878, in the Encyclical "Inscrutabili."   Pius X, in
a *motu proprio* of December 18, 1903, referred to
his "intolerable position"; Benedict XV, in the Encyclical "Pacem," May 23, 1920, reiterated the
protestations; and Pius XI, in his first Encyclical
"Ubi Arcano," December 23, 1922, said:

The true guarantees of liberty . . . which Divine Providence . . . has conferred upon the sovereignty of the Vicar
of Christ here below, which for centuries have fitted in so
marvelously with the Divine designs in order to protect the
liberty of the Roman Pontiff, and for which neither has
Divine Providence itself manifested, nor human ingenuity
as yet discovered, any substitute, . . . these guarantees We
declare have been and are still being violated. Whence it
is that there has been created a certain abnormal condition of affairs which has grievously troubled and up to the
present hour continues to trouble the conscience of the
Catholics of Italy and of the entire world.

We, therefore . . . protest against such a condition of
affairs in defense of the rights and of the dignity of the
Apostolic See, not because We are moved by any vain
earthly ambition of which We should be ashamed, but out
of a sense of Our duty to the dictates of conscience itself.[26]

Because of their refusal the Popes have had to

[26]Ryan, Encyclicals of Pius XI, p. 44.

remain "Prisoners" in the Vatican, prisoners not by physical force but by the force of reason; to have left the Vatican was to accept the Law of Guarantees, and that was an impossibility. The "Question," as it began to be called, was not thus to be solved. And yet that law in its terms uncannily resembles the actual treaty recently signed.

Why did they refuse it? That can be answered in few words: precisely because it was a law, and not a treaty. All these years the Popes have stood ready to accept most of the terms of the Law of Guarantees if they came in treaty form, but not if they were merely a law.

The reason for that position is now clear. The law created only an internal, not an international, situation. It was a unilateral, not a bilateral, document. It was a grant of certain things from the Italian parliament, not a recognition of sovereignty.[27] It was a piece of legislation, changeable by

[27]This was recognized as long ago as 1921, by the liberal paper *Messagero*, which said: "The Law of Guarantees does not recognize as a *right* the sovereignty of the Pontiff, inasmuch as no sovereignty can exist without territory." With remarkable prescience it goes on: "Now the territory necessary to realize the idea of such sovereignty might be within the palace of the Vatican itself" (June 5, 1921).

any legislature. No territory was acknowledged
in which the Pope was sovereign, for the Vatican
palace and grounds were declared an extra-territorial, but not an independent, piece of land. Sovereignty was, therefore, implicitly denied; the instrument of sovereignty, namely, free territory,
was not acknowledged, and to have accepted it was
to renounce his sovereignty, which no Pope was at
liberty to do by virtue of his supreme spiritual mission of the universal care of the souls committed
to him by the Chief Shepherd.

In a word, the Law of Guarantees was refused
precisely because it was an act of a legislature,
passed on a subject of Italy, not a contractual instrument between Italy and a co-equal sovereign.
The Pope was in the unfortunate position of remaining in the Vatican a virtual prisoner, for to go
out was implicitly to accept the Law of Guarantees.

But by the refusal of the Popes an entirely
novel situation was created for the Papacy. I said
above that there were only three means by which
an independent sovereignty could be safeguarded:
possession of sufficient force to repel invasion, an

international agreement to protect it, or at least an acknowledged free, juridical status before international law. Here was the Pope possessing none of these, and yet remaining a sovereign.

The explanation of the anomaly is that a fourth mode of national existence had come into being, that of *protest*. For by protest, and not by any other means, did the Popes protect their precious sovereignty for fifty-nine years. That they did protect it, is evidenced by the fact that in the year 1928, twenty-seven countries had full-fledged diplomatic representatives, ambassadors or ministers plenipotentiary, at the court of the Holy See.[28]

[28]These were: *Ambassadors:* Belgium, Brazil, Chile, Colombia, France, Germany, Peru, Poland and Spain. *Ministers:* Argentina, Austria, Bavaria, Bolivia, Costa Rica, Czechoslovakia, Great Britain, Haiti, Hungary, Jugoslavia, Latvia, Lithuania, Monaco, Nicaragua, Portugal, Rumania, San Marino, and Venezuela. The United States had a Minister to the Holy See from 1848 to 1868. See Moore, Digest of International Law, I, p. 130, for President Polk's interesting instructions to the first chargé d'affaires, Jacob L. Martin, of North Carolina. The last Minister was Rufus King, of Wisconsin (1863-1868). For a full list of the U. S. Ministers, cf. Historical Records and Studies, Vol. XI, December, 1917, pp. 85-88; see also Vol. XII, June, 1918, pp. 115-117. In 1869, President Grant, in his annual message to Congress, recommended that the legation at the Vatican be discontinued. *Catholic Standard and Times* (Philadelphia), Feb. 16, 1929, p. 1.

Since the Pope could not be called a plenary subject of international law, the lawyers invented a
new and exclusive term for his status: they denom-
inated him a subject *sui generis* of international
law, and as such he was entitled to entertain diplomatic relations.[29]

It is clear that such a situation was highly
anomalous and by its very nature impermanent.
Protest has by itself this character, that the longer it is repeated the weaker it grows.   Moreover,
a certain tolerance grew up gradually between the
Holy See and the Quirinal,[30] and this in itself constituted an extreme danger to independence, for
acquiescence in the situation might easily lead to
sanctioning it. The Church could not renounce
its principles, for they were based on its spiritual

[29]Moore, op. cit., I, p. 16 and 39.   Mussolini, in his report on
March 14, 1929, admits the Papacy enjoyed a *de facto* sovereignty
in regard to Italy since 1870. (New York *Times,* March 15, 1929).

[30]Thus the old feud between the "Blacks" and the "Whites", dear
to readers of Marion Crawford, had entirely disappeared (Carrère,
The Pope, pp. 214-5); Pius X practically withdrew the *Non Expedit*
of Pius IX forbidding Catholics to enter public life; there was a
Papal Monsignor as chaplain at the Court of Italy, etc. Pius XI's
appearance on the balcony of St. Peter's the day of his election was
a vast step forward.

mission. And yet year by year it became more difficult to explain them and defend them, since the Papacy seemed very well off as it was. It was long ago decided in Vatican circles that the first favorable opportunity should be taken of coming to an agreement with an Italian Government.

The Pope's position, so far from being satisfactory, as many well-intentioned persons imagined, was actually becoming dangerous. A recent writer, Msgr. Filippo Bernardini, of the Catholic University, and a nephew of Cardinal Gasparri, explains this fact:

The necessity of a solution of the Roman Question, for the Holy See and for Italy, had become more and more apparent every day. The witnesses of the historical events of 1870 have passed away, and the new generation, leaving aside the ideas of a half-hearted tolerance, have gradually become used to the existing state of affairs. Under the inevitable pressure of historical events, and especially of the World War, a new national spirit has arisen. The conception of an Italy, united under Rome as its capital, has been generally accepted as an established fact, the many advantages of which are too evident to be disregarded.

This new viewpoint, common to the clergy and people, has already suggested a *modus vivendi* in the relations of the Church and the State, which, avoiding, as far as possible, all useless contentions, would permit a sufficiently peaceful existence.   This acquiescence in existing conditions has been very dangerous to the principles which the Catholic Church could not renounce, and which, nevertheless, year by year, were becoming more inexplicable to the Catholics of Italy and of the entire world, notwithstanding the repeated and explicit declarations of the Popes.   Hence, the necessity, on the part of the Holy See, of finding an early solution for this so-called Roman Question.[31]

Granted the original proposition that sovereignty is necessary to preserve the Pope's spiritual prerogatives, this position is unassailable.

The opportunity to make it valid in act was long in coming.   It must be admitted that sectarian prejudice and hatred kept Italy from making peace with the Pope.   Freemasonry was in the saddle, and to Freemasonry, Catholicism was *l'infâme*, to be crushed out of existence.   Never, in all the long years from 1870 to the World War, was there a Government in Italy willing, if it was able, to come to terms with the Holy See.   Moreover, Italian Masonry practically did the bidding even in internal affairs of a foreign ministry, that of France,

[31]*Catholic News* (New York), February 23, 1929.

and it was never the policy of France to allow Italy to grow strong[32] as it undoubtedly would if it managed to heal the cancer of dissension that was eating it from within.

But the World War brought an entirely new shuffle of affairs. For the first time it might be said that Italy became truly conscious of unity, for before that it had, as Nitti once said, been still a mere collection of localities, mutually hating or despising one another. That local spirit was burned out in the fires of war, and Italy emerged a nation in very truth. Nobody recognized this more quickly than the Papacy.

This new spirit of unity was not long in bringing about its inevitable reaction, impatience with the mediocrity of Italy's parliamentary rulers since 1870 and with the inefficiency and corruption that followed in their train. Fascism was foreordained to rule Italy from then on. Mussolini saw his chance and the "March on Rome" took its place in history as the last act in a bloodless revolution,

[32]Mussolini made this one of the principal reasons for the law of 1925 against Freemasonry in Italy.

or rather a revolution that shed all its blood in a social civil war before it performed its first political act. The revolution would have happened even had there been no Mussolini. It might have been a Bolshevist revolution.

One of the first things that Mussolini saw was the necessity of settling the religious question. He firmly held the Catholic contention that religion is the prime factor in that moral education of a people to which he himself was so passionately devoted and also the most important element in political unification and tranquil stability. For five years, however, he tried in vain to win the support of this element for his ideal of unity, for every attempt to do so was wrecked by the repeated protests of the Sovereign Pontiff, and his constant reminders not to overlook the fundamental aspect of the Roman Question. Hence, from this position where both the Pope and the Government recognized the necessity of a solution, it was not long before a new step was taken, that of sitting down behind a table and talking terms. In October, 1926, the fateful conferences began.

The Negotiations Begin

IN what has gone before, we have set out all the elements of the question which had to be solved by the conferees. It had first to be accepted by the Italian delegates that the motive of the Pope in desiring sovereignty was a spiritual one, not lust for power and a place in the purely temporal councils of the nations. Pius XI paved the way for this in the beautiful words of his first Encyclical, "Ubi Arcano":

It is scarcely necessary to say here how painful it is to Us to note that from this galaxy of friendly Powers that surround Us one is missing, Italy, Our own dear native land, the country where the hand of God, who guides the course of history, has set down the Chair of His Vicar on Earth. . . .

Then, after setting forth once more the terms of settlement, he said:

; At all events, Italy has not nor will she in the future have anything to fear from the Holy See. The Pope, no matter who he may be, will always repeat the words: "I think thoughts of peace, not of affliction" (Jer. xxix, 11).[33]

It had to be agreed by the Pope that he no longer desired to occupy Rome, to the exclusion of the Italian seat of government. This momentous declaration was made at the very beginning of the negotiations, in the *Osservatore Romano*, to the effect that the Holy See, in demanding territory as the basis of its independent sovereignty would be satisfied with one "however small" (*quantunque piccolo*).[34] On this basis there was no loss to Italy to agree to a recognition of the Pope's sovereignty, and his re-establishment as a temporal sovereign, *de facto*. The Liberal governmental organ, the *Tempo*, had already admitted this on June 2, 1922, when it said:

In order that this long-standing and troublesome "Roman Question" should reach a suitable solution it is necessary for Italian policy to convince itself of this: to hand over to the complete possession of the pontificate the territorial zone which is necessary to it—so that the Holy See

[33]Ryan, Encyclicals of Pius XI, p. 45.

[34]Cf. *America,* Vol. XXXVIII, No. 3, October 29, 1927, Chronicle, s. v. Rome, p. 52; and article, "The Pope's Temporal Power," Wilfrid Parsons, S.J., p. 56.

may stand in the eyes of the whole believing universe perfectly and serenely protected from any interference or predominance on the part of any particular nationality—will not constitute any diminution of the rights of the State.[35]

There remained the problem of the manner in which this recognition might be achieved. To set the Pope up with large lands and great armed forces was not to be thought of. At one time since the War there was question of the second mode of founding his sovereignty, namely, an international treaty of neutrality. This was abandoned in the face of determined Italian opposition.[36] A second declaration in the months following in the *Osservatore Romano* informed the knowing of the progress of negotiations. It was to the effect that the Pope looked on the Roman Question as an internal one for Italy, to be settled between Italy and the Holy See, with no outside intervention. From then on it might be foreseen what form the final settlement would take. Italy would abandon the position

[35]Carrère, op. cit., p. 225.

[36]Mussolini, in his Report of March 14, 1929, says the Holy See never at any time of the negotiations asked for this (New York *Times*, March 16, 1929).

taken in the Law of Guarantees and proceed to make a treaty with the Holy See, as with a co-equal subject of international law. Once this decision was taken, it was merely a matter of working out the multiform details that such a treaty would involve.

The unofficial negotiations began on August 6, 1926, between two laymen, Francesco Pacelli for the Holy See and Professor Domenico Barone for Italy. They both held instructions from the High Parties and saw each other nearly every day. On October 4, Barone was given a letter authorizing him to continue, and on October 6, Pacelli received a like one from Cardinal Gasparri. These two gentlemen at this time held 110 interviews. The first text of the Treaty, in sixteen articles, was ready as long ago as November 24, 1926, but it as yet held only the authority of the two private negotiators.

At the end of 1926, Msgr. Borgongini Duca began to take part in the meetings to work on a Concordat. These lasted until the end of February, 1927, and ended in a new text of both Treaty and Concordat. For over a year this text was studied by the Pope and his consultors and by the Government, and on August 20, 1928, the preliminary work of the original negotiations was done.

On September 3, Pacelli received an order from Cardinal Gasparri, authorizing him to proceed officially in the name of the Holy See; on November 22, Barone received a like one from the King, while on November 25 Pacelli was authorized by the Holy Father himself. The health of Barone was failing rapidly and on January 4 he died a holy death. On January 21, Mussolini himself took the place of his dead representative in successive meetings, while every evening Pacelli related to the Pope what he had done that day, and received fresh instructions.[37]

[37]This whole "inside story" of the negotiations was told by the papal representative, Signor Pacelli, in an interview in the *Popolo d'Italia,* of Milan, February 14, 1929, which I have followed. An interesting sidelight of his story involves the Chicago Eucharistic Congress of June, 1926. He was one of Cardinal Bonzano's suite on that occasion. It was during the Congress, he tells us, that he had an interior conviction that God was shortly to bring about a solution of the Roman Question. He mentioned this, however, to nobody. His conviction became stronger as he approached home on

©Internatl. Newsreel.

The Signing of the Treaty, February 11, 1929.

Signor Pacelli tells us that during these last anxious days the Pope prayed incessantly, and we know that he had holy persons all over the world interceding for him at the throne of God. During all these negotiations the three documents went through twenty revisions. As is known, when the last touch was put to them, there was no hesitation. The three documents were signed at the Lateran Palace by Cardinal Gasparri for the Holy See and the Hon. Benito Mussolini for the King, on February 11, 1929, Feast of Our Lady of Lourdes. They had later to be presented to the Italian Grand Council, which was done on March 14, and to the Parliament, for ratification, and later to be signed by the Pope and the King. These documents were: (1) the Treaty settling the Roman Question, (2) the Concordat regulating the relations of Church and State in Italy, and (3) the Financial Convention.

the ocean liner and it was with almost no surprise that shortly after his arrival he received a call from Professor Barone to ask him upon what conditions the Holy See would be willing to entertain a solution of the Question. Was the settlement one of the graces of the Congress?

The Question Is Settled

THE striking thing about the Treaty, as distinct from the Concordat, is its extreme simplicity. The anguishing Question, which all the world had declared to be insoluble, is settled by less than 200 words. That in itself is a tribute to the justice of the Papal position. The gist of the settlement is contained in three articles: (1) recognition of the sovereignty of the Pope over the so-called "City of the Vatican" (Article 2), (2) a recognition of Vatican City as territory independent of Italy (Article 3), (3) the abolition of the Law of Guarantees on the part of Italy and the declaration by the Pope that by the present treaty the Roman Question is finally and irrevocably settled (Article 26). The intervening articles are the inevitable details, and are here summarized.[38]

As was said, there are three documents. The first, the Treaty proper, establishes the independ-

[38]See Appendix A., p. 81, for the texts.

ence of the Holy See; it comprises a preamble and twenty-seven articles. The Concordat is similar in form to the many other agreements made with various countries, and comprises a preamble and forty-five articles. The financial convention comprises three articles.

To make clear the difference between the first two of these documents, we cannot do better than to quote their preambles, which state the reason for their existence.

The preamble to the Treaty reads:

IN THE NAME OF THE MOST HOLY TRINITY:

Whereas the Holy See and Italy have recognized the convenience of eliminating every reason for difference existing between them, to come to a definite arrangement of their reciprocal relations conforming to justice and the dignity of the two high parties and assuring to the Holy See in a stable way the condition of fact and of right which guarantees to it absolute independence in fulfilment of its high mission in the world, and by which the Holy See consents to recognize the Roman Question raised in 1870 with the assigning of Rome to the Kingdom of Italy under the dynasty of the House of Savoy as settled in an irrevocable manner: and

Whereas, owing to the necessity of assuring absolute visible independence to the Holy See, in order to guarantee to it indisputable sovereignty also in the international field, it is deemed necessary to constitute Vatican City with special dispositions, recognizing its full property rights with exclusive and absolute power and sovereign jurisdiction over it to the Holy See; His Holiness, the Supreme Pontiff, Pius XI, and his Majesty Victor Emmanuel III, King of Italy, have resolved to stipulate a treaty, etc.

The preamble to the Concordat reads:

IN THE NAME OF THE MOST HOLY TRINITY:
Whereas since the beginning of the negotiations between the Holy See and Italy for resolution of the Roman Question, the Holy See itself has proposed that a treaty relative to the said question should be accompanied as a necessary complement by a concordat for settling the conditions of religion and the Church in Italy, and

Whereas a treaty for solution of the Roman Question has been concluded and signed today; His Holiness, etc.

In other words, the Treaty is a special instrument arising from the peculiar position of the Holy See in Italy, while the Concordat is the usual agreement of which the Holy See has made many with countries where there is a large number of Catholics and where it is necessary to agree beforehand so that all possible difficulties may be foreseen and any conflict between Church and State may be avoided.

The first four articles of the Treaty contain general principles. In Article one, Italy recognizes again Article I of the Constitution whereby the Catholic religion is the sole religion of the State. Note that it says "sole religion *of* the State," not the sole religion *in* the State. Religious freedom is guaranteed by the Constitution, and that is not changed by this Treaty. This was explicitly stated by Mussolini on March 14, 1929.[39] Italy also (Article two) recognizes the sovereignty of the Holy See as a national entity "as an inherent attribute of its nature, in conformity with its tradition and the exigencies of its mission in the world." Article three sets up Vatican City, leaving the Piazza of St. Peter open to the public, and allowing the Italian police to preserve order in it on certain occasions.[40] Article four is the usual guaran-

[39]New York *Times,* March 15, 1929.

[40]By article five of the Treaty the whole of Vatican City is to be enclosed, except the Piazza of St. Peter's. By an unusual concession in international law, the Piazza is ordinarily to be open and policed by the Italian State, "whose authority will cease at the foot of the steps leading into the Basilica." The Holy See reserves the right to close the Piazza to Italy on days of special ceremony. (Article three).

tee of mutual non-interference in each other's affairs.

It is the second Article which differentiates the Treaty from the Law of Guarantees and makes it a document which the Pope could accept. He is not merely granted the *use* of the Vatican and its grounds, as did the Law, but it is recognized as his, not in the form of an owner under the crown of Italy, but in the manner of an independent sovereign. This land is cut out of Italy and made foreign territory. In this territory, then, the Pope is acknowledged to be sovereign in every sense of the word.

Thus the principle for which five Popes had contended is at last acknowledged. The manner of the solution in its final form is so simple that one almost catches oneself wondering why it should have been so long in coming. This is ever the character of great events. It is rather the clearing-away of previous prejudices and ambitions that takes time. When this is done, and the deed stands forth in all its naked purity, it needs no argument or defense; it is its own justification.

Articles five, six and seven are necessary regulations having to do with present tenants in the territory of the Holy See, with water supply, railroad communications, telephone, telegraph, radio and cable, all of which are furnished by Italy at its own expense. In Article seven Italy agrees not to allow new constructions nearby overlooking Vatican City, and forbids aircraft to fly over it.[41]

The person of the Sovereign Pontiff is sacred (Article eight). Attempts against his life, or propaganda to commit them will be punished by Italy, and offenses and insults against him in written and spoken word will not be allowed, as too often was not the case in the past. Thus we will now be spared the unpardonable outrages which have disgraced the American name in the past.

Three other articles, nine, ten and twenty-one, specify the subjects of Vatican City, the rights of Cardinals, who will receive the honors of princes of the blood, and certain liberties of Vatican offi-

[41]Contrary to first press dispatches, no disposition will be made on Vatican territory for Papal aircraft, nor would there be room. Article six of the Treaty provides that agreements will be made for the circulation on Italian territory of land vehicles and aircraft of Vatican City.

cials living in Rome itself. Similarly, diplomatic agents accredited to the Holy See receive immunity if living in Rome, and Italy and the Holy See agree to exchange ambassadors. The Holy Father, according to reports, will name Msgr. Borgongini Duca as his first legate to Italy, a well-deserved honor. Passport arrangements are made in Article nineteen and freedom from Italian customs for Vatican merchandise is decreed in Article twenty. Usual extradition agreements are made for criminal fugitives, and by request of the Holy See, Italy will judge and punish crimes committed in Vatican City (Articles twenty-two and three).

Articles thirteen to sixteen concern properties and property rights. Three kinds of Vatican properties are named: those in Vatican City, over which the Holy See has ownership and sovereignty; those in Italian territory to which diplomatic immunity or extra-territoriality are granted by Italy; and those which are declared tax exempt.[42] In the

[42]A significant concession in property rights is contained in Article twenty-eight of the Concordat: *"In order to appease the conscience of those who under Italian law own ecclesiastical property, the Holy See grants full recognition to the title of such property. The Holy See will advise Bishops to that effect."*

second category fall various churches and office buildings owned by the Pope and in the third are the Gregorian University, the Biblical, Oriental and Archeological Institutes and a few other places.

The Treaty ends with the solemn declaration by the Pope that he is satisfied that by it he has been assured the requisite independence for the pursuit of his spiritual functions, that he now at last recognizes the legitimacy of the dynasty of Savoy on the throne of Italy, and that he declares the Roman Question forever eliminated (Article twenty-six).

The Concordat which follows will appear to those who are not familiar with such instruments as a remarkable document. As a matter of fact there is much in it which is new, especially some matters peculiar to Italy, and the regulations on marriage and education, which go far beyond former concordats in their generosity and will no doubt be a model for future ones with other States. The very making of a concordat is a frank recognition that there do exist fields in which the interests of Church and State overlap, and hence which might possibly become sources of conflict in the future. The purpose is to foresee and eliminate these as far as possible, and to provide for an amicable settlement of any disagreements which may arise. The Concordat with Italy is an extraordinary object lesson for the world. It is hard to see, if its terms are respected, how any possible religious disputes can hereafter arise. It is the fruit of centuries of experience.

It is not necessary to detail all its provisions here. It arranges, for instance, for freedom of worship (Article one); freedom of communication and of the publication of religious notices (Article two); and freedom of association (Articles twenty-nine to thirty-one).

Articles three to eight detail the rights and duties of clerics in their civic capacity. Some of these are interesting. Theological students and novices in Religious Orders are not exempt from military training but may put it off until their twenty-sixth year. All clerics in orders are exempt from the army, except in a general mobilization, when they will be assigned "preferentially" to the hospital service, and all parish priests and their assistants are exempt even then.[43] All ecclesiastics are exempt from jury duty. No ecclesiastic may join a political party as an actual member in the European sense, but ecclesiastics may hold State and municipal positions with the permission of their superiors and they lose their position if this permission is withdrawn. No apostate priest or one under censure may hold any teaching position or wear the ecclesiastical garb. It is to be noted that Article seven protects the seal of Confession legally.[44]

Some of the regulations have a special interest. Thus the ten holy days of the Church are made legal holidays (Article eleven). All Bishops before taking office will take an oath before the Premier to respect the King and Government under the Constitution, and to abstain from doing anything

[43]However, Article three of the Concordat provides that all clerics conscripted retain the right to wear their cassocks or Religious habits, "so that they can practise among the troops their sacred ministry."

[44]The early press report hinted that clerics violating Italian laws would enjoy the *privilegium fori*, that is, would be tried by a court of their own ecclesiastical peers. The contrary is the fact. See Article eight of the Concordat, Appendix A, pp. 97-98.

to injure the Italian State or public peace (Article twenty). Ownership of the Catacombs is vested in the Holy See, with freedom to excavate (Article thirty-three). Papal titles of nobility are recognized by Italy (Articles forty-one and two). The societies grouped under the name of "Catholic Action" are recognized by Italy, since their activities are non-political (Article forty-three). This article was undoubtedly the object of especial solicitude by the Holy Father. By Article twelve liturgical prayers are ordered for the King and State, at High Mass in churches where there is a Chapter.

Article twenty-nine has especial interest for Italy. By it, all of the tyrannical and unjust legislation passed by the anti-clerical Governments of Italy is repealed, especially as regards Religious Orders, Congregations, sodalities, confraternities, etc. By these laws, most of them passed before 1870, their rights of association, of corporate ownership, of public meeting, of exemption from taxation, and their general juridical status, were severely limited, for alleged political reasons. The hard common sense of present-day Italy, free from the sectarian slogans of other days, has recognized that these societies, far from being enemies of the State, are among its precious allies, in preserving the high moral idealism which is the foundation of good citizenship.

Very intricate regulations are made with regard to the setting-up of parishes and dioceses (Articles sixteen to eighteen) and to the appointment of Bishops and beneficed clergy (Articles nineteen to twenty-six). It is sufficient to remark that the old royal prerogatives of the *exequatur* and the *placet*, by which Kings controlled the hierarchy, and those concerning benefices, are abolished. The choice of Bishops is declared to belong to the Holy See, but before their appointment the latter will communicate their names to the Government "in order to be sure that the Government has no objections of a political nature" against them. This is a reasonable concession.

Article thirty-four concerns marriage. Italy now recognizes the Sacrament of Matrimony and the religious marriage has civil effect, as in the United States, though civil marriage for those who

wish it alone is not abolished.[45] There is no divorce,
as heretofore, and declarations of nullity because
of a defect in the marriage contract, pertain to
ecclesiastical courts, and will be decided according
to canon law.   In this way, all those disagreements over marriage common to modern countries
will be completely eliminated.

Finally, education is treated in Articles thirty-
five to forty.   As heretofore, Christian doctrine
must be taught in primary schools, but this provision is extended now to secondary schools as well.
Teachers of Christian doctrine, clerical as well as
lay, will be certificated by the Bishop of the place,
and only textbooks approved by the ecclesiastical
authorities will be used.   Religious instruction of
the "Balilla," or boys' physical-education societies,
is also provided for.   Seminaries and colleges for
Church training are exempt from Government interference, but all other educational institutions

[45]The preamble to this Article is worth quoting here: "The
Italian State, wishing to reinvest the institution of marriage, which
is the basis of the family, with the dignity conformable to the Catholic traditions of its people, recognizes the Sacrament of Matrimony
performed according to canon law as fully effective in civil law."
There is in these few words a whole treatise on modern problems.

are subject to the Government examinations for recognition of their degrees.

The third document signed by the plenipotentiaries was the Financial Convention. It consists of only three articles (see Appendix A).

The very Law of Guarantees passed by those who dispossessed the Pope recognized that there was due to him a material restitution for what they had done. For this they purposed to pay him in perpetuity an annuity of 3,225,000 lire, a large sum in those days. It was refused. If it had been accepted, it would have amounted up to date to 187,050,000 gold lire. Instead of this sum, which the enemies of the Church thought due, the Pope receives 1,550,000,000 lire, or about 400,000,000 gold lire ($77,200,000). He takes it in the following form: 1,000,000,000 lire in Italian 5 per cent State bonds par value (about 800,000,000 lire market value at present) and 750,000,000 in bank credits. Mussolini, in his report of March 15, 1929, to the Grand Council, expressed himself as particularly gratified to note the Pope's confidence in the stability of Italian State securities.

There has, fortunately, been no disposition in responsible quarters to criticize this arrangement. It falls far below the value of the original injury in lands and other property taken. It is then, from this point of view, merely a matter of returning to the Church some of what was taken from it. It will be applied to defray some of the expenses incurred in the central administration of a Church which numbers more than 300,000,000 people. The remainder of those expenses will continue, as in the past, to be made up by free contributions of the Faithful, in what is called "Peter's Pence," a form of donation which dates back to the dim Middle Ages.

No doubt, many will be surprised by the thoroughness and far-reaching character of these agreements. They will not be understood except by those who know something of the character and tradition of the Italians. Even to those who do, it comes as a most welcome surprise that every possible ground of disagreement between a Church and a State which have the same subjects has been previously eliminated in such a spirit of give-and-take. It will not, we hope, be lost on those gloomy persons who foresee nothing but conflict every time there is set up what they are pleased to call union of Church and State.

Implications and Misconceptions

THE implications of the Treaty are vast and complicated. The most startling, so important that it really deserves the much-abused name of historical, is one, strangely enough, that almost escaped the notice of commentators. It is nothing more nor less than that the Popes, after holding it in fact or by right for fifteen hundred years, have irrevocably and freely abdicated their immemorial right to the city of Rome. Greater far in its meaning than the loss of Temporal Power in 1870, and worthy to be classed with the original gift in 754, is this fact. Papal Rome! The blood that has been shed for it, the memories that cluster around it, the precious treasures that it contains, have been handed over to the Italian people for their undisputed possession. It will be long, perhaps, before we are able to realize what that means.

The second consequence of the Treaty, hardly

less important, and almost as little noticed, is that the unity of Italy, a process begun in 1848, is at last a fact. Up to February 11, its very capital was held under protest from its former owner, who still persisted in calling its loss a robbery. The Papal States were occupied by a foreign prince and the rightful sovereign had never recognized his occupation as legitimate. Now by a deliberate contract, his legitimate possession is established, his title to Rome as his capital has a cloud on it no longer, and the Italian people are freed from the incubus of a divided allegiance which weighed so heavily on it, and poisoned much of its social and political life.

The third fact that is most worthy of notice in the settlement is the tininess of the new Papal State. It is this, more than anything else that makes clear the declaration of the Pope that his motive in seeking temporal sovereignty was spiritual and nothing else. Leo XIII, in his vivacious way, had long ago settled this point forever:

Men dare to state [he said in an allocution to Cardinal Alimonda and some Italian priests] that the vindication of the Pope's rights is dictated by a spirit of ambition and worldly grandeur . . . Our aim scales far loftier heights than that, it is the very cause of our liberty and independence that we espouse.[46]

It is a paradox of the situation that in order to enjoy spiritual independence and sovereignty, it was necessary that the Pope be a temporal sovereign. It is clear that to be really free to exercise his religious mission, so that the members of the Church all over the world should clearly apprehend that freedom, the Pope must be the subject of no earthly sovereign. It is equally clear now to those who are not members of the Church that possession of territory for itself was not what was sought, since the Pope was content with little more than he has actually possessed since 1870! This, as Count dalla Torre says so finely, is "that least strip of material territory from which the spiritual cannot prescind here on earth."

Finally, it must be noticed that by the treaty a really clever guarantee has been given the Popes that they will continue to enjoy their independence,

[46]See Appendix B, p. 118.

no matter what changes take place in the government of Italy.[47] The only justifying pretext for the taking of Rome was the political necessity of Italians owning their own natural capital. It was claimed that the Pope stood in the way of a just aspiration of the Italian people and as doing this he must be sacrificed. This pretext is forever removed. What the Pope will hold in actual land, he has already held with Italy's unity unimpaired; his territory is a menace to nobody, and no reasonable pretext will ever be forged to take it away from him. Only pure malice will ever be able to justify Italy again dethroning the Pope, and that will bring upon it the reprobation of the whole world.

It remains to brush away some of the misconceptions that have grown up since the treaty was signed.

The first of these has to do with the position of Catholics throughout the world, those, that is, who are not actually residents in the Vatican and its grounds. There has arisen the grotesque notion

[47]See Appendix B, p. 130.

that these 300,000,000 people have by a stroke of the pen lost their own citizenship and acquired a new one in the 160 acres owned by the Pope, or at least had forced on them a dual allegiance, that to their own country and that to the Pope.[48]

Such a charge is material for popular controversy, but not for reasonable men. Nothing whatever has happened except to those who actually will be registered as habitual residents in the Vatican. For all others the Pope will remain in the same position he has always occupied; he is their supreme spiritual superior and nothing else. Nothing that he could not do to them before can he do now. Their relations with him were of a spiritual nature and they are unchanged. This fact is almost too clear to devote the space to it, were it not for the fact that it has actually been questioned by those who have not clearly apprehended what really did happen by the Treaty.

The settlement has also been attacked on the grounds that union of Church and State is an obsolete doctrine, relegated by all modern peoples to

[48]*Christian Advocate* (New York), Feb. 21, 1929, p. 237.

forgotten limboes. Apart from the fact that the time element does not enter into the truth of a doctrine, a common fallacy, this also is based on a misconception. If it means anything at all, it means that Mussolini and Cardinal Gasparri, in signing the treaty, committed a wrong. A wrong against what? Against other peoples who do not practise union of Church and State? Hardly. It is none of their business. Against an abstract opinion, held by some people, though not by all? But in political theory nobody is at liberty to prescribe to a sovereign nation what form of government it shall adopt for itself, or agree to in another. The very people who utter that objection are those who are most outspoken against our interferences in the nations of Latin America. Even to object to monarchy in another country in the name of liberty is a denial of liberty.

But is there not something especially heinous in the head of a Church enjoying the rights of a sovereign king? If there were, we should have to take up the cudgels against the King of England, who has been head of a church for 400 years. One becomes suspicious that the objection has dwindled down to objecting only to the head of the Catholic Church receiving royal honors, even though it has been made clear a thousand times that these same honors exist merely for the purpose of protecting his spiritual independence, as a practical necessity for a universal religion in a world divided into nations.

The last fallacy of any importance that needs to be pointed out is that the Pope by this new act acquires an international importance which will cause him to interfere in the purely temporal affairs of the world and make him a menace to free peoples. This charge was uttered before the actual treaty was published. Now that it has seen the light, there is no longer any justice in making it. For by Article twenty-four the following is agreed:

The Holy See, in relation to the sovereignty due to it also in the international sphere, declares that it wishes to remain and will remain extraneous to all temporal disputes between States and to international congresses held for such objects, unless the contending parties make concordant appeal to its peaceful mission; at the same time reserving the right to exercise its moral and spiritual power *(la sua potestà morale e spirituale).* In consequence of this, the territory of Vatican City will be considered neutral and inviolable territory.

It has been questioned if this article excludes the Holy See from the League of Nations. It does more than that, it excludes it from any conference of Powers and nations that is discussing purely international matters of State. Moreover we have the authoritative statement of the *Civiltà Cattolica* on this subject. After explaining why the Holy See did not demand an international guarantee for its sovereignty, namely, because such a guarantee would be out of place in a purely spiritual power, it continues:

For a similar reason it has never agreed, nor would it ever agree, to enter the League of Nations, however inspired this might be by the reasonable and Christian purpose of bringing peace among nations. This would be true if for no other reason than that, being by its nature supranational and universal, the Church could never consent to one of the conditions for entering the League, namely, to take part in war and other punitive sanctions against transgressor nations.[49]

[49]*Civiltà Cattolica,* 16 Febbraio, 1929, p. 301.

Thus by the very terms of the treaty, as well as by its universal spiritual character, the Church is protected against the accusation of using its lofty position to further the aims of any selfish national interests.

It is clear enough, then, that most of the adverse comment aroused has been inspired by an unfortunate ignorance of the actual purpose of the Treaty. This ignorance, alas, has not been confined to those who are not Catholics. In Appendix B, Count dalla Torre tells in his eloquent fashion how Pius X struggled against the unfortunate connotation of the words "Temporal Power." He attributes the use of this term, which the Popes themselves never employed, to enemies of the Church who wished by it to obscure and discredit the Pope's actual aims. It is true that the use of sovereignty involves the use of civil government, but both in aim and in execution there is a world of difference between civil government as it exists in the nations of the world and as it is exercised by the Popes.

First of all, the *aim* is different. Government in

all countries is exercised for the purpose of protecting the citizens of those countries, promoting their welfare and safeguarding their interests from outside interference. The subjects of the Pope are not the prime object of his government; its prime object is his own independence, solely that he may be unhampered in the pursuit of his vocation, which is to teach the Revelation of Christ and promote the eternal welfare of all men. This is the first divergence from the ordinary idea of government as it obtains in the nations.

Secondly, the *subjects* of his government are different. In any State the citizen comes first; the family is the unit-basis of the nation. Government exists to protect them. In the Papacy the subjects are the employes of a palace, a museum, a garden, an observatory and a church, about 300 in all. They are not natural subjects, having their roots in any soil, but voluntary ones, mostly brought in for the various services required. This makes a profound difference in the mode of governing.

Thirdly, in the *means* which will be employed

to carry on his government, the Pope will differ widely from the Kings and Premiers of the earth. There will be no army, no police, no departments for any purpose except what exist already for the running of the palace, church and museum services, and for the spiritual government of the universal Church. There will be none of the usual trappings of government in its civil phases, for there will be need of none. His "State" will consist of 160 acres. The Pope voluntarily chose to restrict his territory to the least possible, for this purpose, that the spiritual reason for his independence and sovereignty may be manifest to all.[50]

Fourthly, in the *international* field there will be the widest difference. There will be no defensive and offensive alliances, no treaties except Concordats, which are for the sole purpose of safeguarding the spiritual interests of the Catholic religion. The ordinary diplomacy of the nations, the jockeying for markets, predominance, prestige, spheres of influence, etc., will have no place in

[50]Discourse of Pius XI to the Lenten Preachers. *(Civiltà Cattolica,* ibid., p. 292a).

the international relations of the Church, which has a Divine, not a material, an eternal, not a temporal vocation.

No one has the right, therefore, to say that this is a purely temporal matter and that therefore everyone is free to think what he wants about it. If one is "liberal," runs this idea, one is free to think and to say that the Pope has made a mistake. This is itself a gross mistake, based on a complete misunderstanding of what has really happened. It is not a temporal thing which has happened, but a spiritual; the Pope, in making peace with Italy, has acted for the good of religion in Italy, and therefore of religion the world over. It would be sad for Catholics, at least, to be blinded to this fact. The religious value of independence for the Head of the Church is so enormous that it will be long before the world realizes how great this is.

What of the Future?

WHAT then of the future? Will the Church be really better off than it has been the last fifty years? Will the cause of religion really prosper because of the recognition of sovereignty once more in the Papacy?

With regard to Italy there can be but one answer, an affirmative. One has only to recall the situation which existed to be assured of this fact. For Italians the most potent force in this world had come between them and their duty to God, and that is patriotism. A passionate love of their own land was vitiated at its source by the gnawing knowledge that that land was living in the state of sin. It had perpetrated a robbery for which it had never made restitution. It existed as an individual nation in the very house which it had stolen, not from some person or country like themselves, but from the Head of their own Church.

It is true that this feeling had largely abated

in recent years, that many of the younger generation never adverted to the anomalous state of religion in the country. That was perhaps a worse state than an acute sense of guilt. We have perhaps some inkling of what must now be the feelings of the Italian people, if we reflect on the overwhelming sense of joy that comes to a sinner after confession and absolution from a sin that has lain long unconfessed and unshriven, especially a sin that an apparently ineluctable necessity has driven him to commit. It is truly the dawn of a new day for Italy.

In attempting to understand this, we must not confuse things with what we experience in this country. Here, we are from the beginning accustomed to a variety of religions, most of them calling themselves Christian, but few of them having anything to do with integral Christianity. All sorts and conditions of people and religions exist here side by side. We are used to that, and let them live. We make what external allowances are necessary, and each goes his way in peace. That is a condition of civic concord.

But Italy is totally different. The people are ninety-nine per cent Catholic. Their religious and civic relations are so inextricably commingled, and have been so for centuries, that for the State and the Church to be at loggerheads is like war in the family. Great loyalty to religion exposed its subject to the imputation of a kind of treason to the State, or at the best of lukewarmness. It was hard to be a patriotic citizen without losing at least some attachment to one's religion. This sore in the body politic was rubbed hard with vinegar by interested politicians now and then. The fact that it was really there, was a danger to both Church and State in Italy. And of course nobody will even remotely understand it, if he persists in reading Italy in terms of conditions in the United States. What was an anomaly in Italy, and quite a dangerous one, might very well seem quite normal here, and safe enough.

This anomaly has been removed by the Treaty and Concordat, and Italy has resumed a normal existence. It is clear that both nation and Church cannot but profit by it.

As for religion in the rest of the world, there will, of course, be divergent opinions. Those who think Catholicism to be a distortion of Christianity will be alarmed and pained to see the Pope relieved of an incubus to the free exertion of his activities. There will be attempts to obscure the issue by throwing up the temporal side of the settlement to hide the spiritual side of it, which is the essential.

But anyone who accepts the force of the argument here set forth cannot but rejoice that the settlement has come about. Anyone who feels the cogency of that triple logical link of the necessity of independence for a universal spiritual power, of sovereignty as the sole possible guarantee of independence, and of territory as the sole possible earthly condition of exercising sovereignty, must necessarily rejoice. If the universal Church is hampered by the loss of independence, then it cannot but be good that it has regained the sovereignty that guarantees that independence.

Shortly after his election, Pope Pius XI delivered his famous Encyclical "On the Peace of Christ

in the Kingdom of Christ" ("Ubi Arcano").
Speaking of the possibility of a reconciliation with
Italy, he said:

It is God's task to bring about this happy hour and to
make it known to all; men of wisdom and of good will sure-
ly will not permit it to strike in vain. When it does arrive,
it will be a solemn hour, full of happy consequences not
only for the restoration of the Kingdom of Christ, but for
the pacification of Italy and the world as well.[51]

That solemn hour has come, and no Christian
can sincerely do aught than thank God for it.

[51]Ryan, Encyclicals of Pius XI, p. 46.

Appendix A

Text of the Treaty, Concordat and Financial Convention.

[Note: This translation of the documents is the property of the United Press Associations, and is here reprinted by permission.]

I

THE TREATY

IN THE NAME OF THE MOST HOLY TRINITY:

Whereas the Holy See and Italy have recognized the convenience of eliminating every reason for difference existing between them, to come to a definite arrangement of their reciprocal relations, which conforms to the justice and to the dignity of the two high parties, and assuring to the Holy See in a stable way the condition of fact and of right which guarantees to it absolute independence in fulfillment of its high mission to the world, and by which the Holy See consents to recognize the Roman question raised in 1870 with the assigning of Rome to the Kingdom of Italy under the dynasty of the House of Savoy as settled in an irrevocable manner: and

Whereas, owing to the necessity to assure absolute visible independence to the Holy See in order to guarantee it indisputable sovereignty also in the international field, it is deemed necessary to constitute Vatican City with special dispositions, recognizing its full property rights, with exclusive and absolute power and sovereign jurisdiction over it to the Holy See; his Holiness, the Supreme Pontiff, Pius XI., and his Majesty, Victor Emmanuel III., King of Italy, have resolved to stipulate a treaty, nominating two plenipotentiaries for this purpose, namely, on the part of his Holiness, his Most Reverend Eminence Cardinal Pietro Gasparri, his Secretary of State, and on the part of his Majesty, Signor Cavaliere Benito Mussolini, President of the Cabinet, and chief of the Government, who, having exchanged their respective credentials, found the same good and in due form, have agreed to the following articles:

ARTICLE ONE

Italy recognizes and reaffirms the principle set forth in Article I of the Constitution of the Kingdom of Italy of March 4, 1848, whereby the Roman Catholic Apostolic religion is the sole religion of the State.

ARTICLE TWO

Italy recognizes the sovereignty of the Holy See in the international field as an inherent attribute of its nature, in conformity with its tradition and the exigencies of its mission in the world.

ARTICLE THREE

Italy recognizes full possession and exclusive and absolute power and sovereign jurisdiction of the Holy See over the Vatican, as at present constituted, with all its appurtenances and endowments, creating Vatican City for such purpose with its special aims in connection with the present treaty. The confines of said Vatican City are indicated on a plan which constitutes the first annex to the present treaty, and of which it forms an integral part. It is agreed, however, that St. Peter's Square, also forming a part of Vatican City, will continue ordinarily to be open to the public and subject to the police powers of Italian authority, which authority will cease at the foot of the steps leading into the basilica, although the latter will continue to be destined for public worship. The police will abstain, therefore, from ascending the steps or approaching the basilica, except in case they should be invited to enter by competent authorities. When the Holy See, in expectation of a special ceremony, will deem it opportune to withdraw St. Peter's Square from free public transit, the Italian authorities, unless invited by competent authorities to remain, will retire beyond the external lines of the Bernini colonnade and its prolongation.

ARTICLE FOUR

The sovereignty and exclusive jurisdiction which Italy recognizes to the Holy See implies that there cannot be any interference whatsoever on the part of the Italian Government, and that within Vatican City there will be no other authority than the Holy See.

ARTICLE FIVE

For the execution of that which is established in the preceding article, before the present treaty goes into effect, the territory constituting Vatican City must be made free from all liens or any eventual tenants by the Italian Government. The Holy See will provide for closing the approaches by inclosing the open part except St. Peter's Square. It is, however, agreed that regarding real estate therein belonging to religious institutions or organizations, the Holy See will arrange directly to regulate its relations with these, the Italian State being disinterested.

ARTICLE SIX

Italy undertakes to furnish through agreement with Interested organizations assurance to Vatican City of an adequate supply of water within the territory. It will also provide for communication with Italian State railroads by constructing a railroad station within Vatican City at a location marked on the annexed plan, as well as for the movement of the Vatican's coaches on Italian railroads. It will also provide direct connection of telephone services, telegraphs, radio telephones, radio and postal telegraph with other States to Vatican City. It will, besides, provide for coordination of other public services. The Italian State will furnish the above at its own expense within one year from the date the present treaty goes into effect. The Holy See will arrange at its own expense for systematizing the present approaches to the Vatican, as well as others which it thinks it may be necessary to open. Agreements will be made between the Holy See and the Italian Government for circulation in the latter's territory of land vehicles and aircraft of Vatican City.

ARTICLE SEVEN

In territory surrounding Vatican City the Italian Government pledges not to permit new construction which overlooks Vatican City. It will also provide for the partial demolition, for the same purpose, of those already existing at Porta Cavalleggeri and along the Via Aurelia and Viale Vaticano.

In conformity with the regulations of international law, aircraft of any kind are prohibited from flying over Vatican territory. In Rusticucci Square and zones adjacent to the colonnade, where extraterritoriality does not extend according to Article fifteen, any building or street changes which might interest the Vatican must be made by common accord.

ARTICLE EIGHT

Italy considers the person of the Supreme Pontiff as sacred and inviolate, and declares attempts against him, or propaganda to commit them, punishable by the same penalties established for attempts or propaganda to commit them against the person of the King. Offenses or insults publicly committed in Italian territory against the person of the Supreme Pontiff with spoken or written word are punishable as such offenses or insults against the person of the King.

ARTICLE NINE

In conformity with the regulations of international law, all persons having fixed residences in Vatican City are subject to the sovereignty of the Holy See. Such residence is not lost by the simple fact of temporary residence elsewhere when not accompanied by the loss of a house in Vatican City or by other circumstances showing abandonment of residence.

Ceasing to be subject to the sovereignty of the Holy See, persons mentioned in the preceding paragraph will be considered outright Italian citizens in Italy, when not in possession of other citizenship. The same persons, while subject to the sovereignty of the Holy See, will be subject in Italian territory—even in matters wherein personal law must be observed—to Italian legislation, and in cases where they are believed to be citizens of other countries they shall be subject to the laws of the State to which they belong.

Article Ten

Dignitaries of the church and persons belonging to the pontifical court, who will be designated in a list to be agreed upon by the high contracting parties, even when not citizens of the Vatican, will always in all cases regarding Italy be exempt from military service, from jury duty, and from all services of a personal character. This rule also will be applied to functionaries declared by the Holy See to be indispensable and those permanently attached with fixed stipends to offices of the Holy See, and also to departments and offices designated and assigned in Articles thirteen, fourteen, fifteen and sixteen existing outside Vatican City.

Such functionaries will be listed by agreement as the above-mentioned list is brought up to date annually by the Holy See. Ecclesiastics who for reasons of their offices are occupied outside Vatican City in execution of acts of the Holy See will not be subject by reason of their offices to any impediment, investigation or molestation on the part of the Italian authorities. Every foreigner invested with ecclesiastical office will enjoy the same personal guaranties due to Italian citizens by virtue of the laws of the Kingdom.

ARTICLE ELEVEN

The central bodies of the Catholic Church are exempt from all interference on the part of the Italian State, except for dispositions of Italian law concerning purchases by moral bodies, as well as transfer of real estate.

ARTICLE TWELVE

Italy recognizes to the Holy See the active and passive right to maintain legations according to the general regulations of international law. Envoys of foreign Governments to the Holy See will continue to enjoy all of the prerogatives and immunities which accrue to diplomatic agents according to international law. Their seats can continue to remain in Italian territory, enjoying the immunity due them according to international law, even though their States shall not have diplomatic relations with Italy. It is agreed that Italy pledges forever in every case to let pass freely correspondence of all States, including belligerents, both to the Holy See and vice versa, as well as to permit free access of Bishops of the whole world to the Apostolic See.

The high contracting parties pledge themselves to establish normal diplomatic relations through the accrediting of an Italian ambassador to the Holy See and of a pontifical nuncio to Italy, who will be dean of the diplomatic corps according to the customary right recognized by the Congress of Vienna, January 9, 1815.

By reason of the recognized sovereignty, and without prejudice as set forth in Article nineteen, diplomats and

Holy See couriers sent in the name of the Supreme Pontiff enjoy in Italian territory, even in time of war, the same treatment due diplomats and diplomatic carriers of other foreign Governments according to the regulations of international law.

ARTICLE THIRTEEN

Italy recognizes to the Holy See the full possession of the patriarchal basilicas of St. John Lateran, of St. Mary the Greater, and of St. Paul Outside the Walls, with their annexed buildings. The State transfers to the Holy See free direction and administration of the basilica of St. Paul and also its annexed monastery, paying the Holy See sums corresponding to the amounts fixed annually by the Ministry of Education for said edifice. It is at the same time agreed that the Holy See is in freehold possession of the edifice of St. Calixtus, near St. Mary in Trastevere.

ARTICLE FOURTEEN

Italy recognizes to the Holy See full property rights of the pontifical palace of Castel Gandolfo, with all endowments and appurtenances which at present are possessed by the Holy See, as well as pledging itself to cede the same terms in full property rights of the Villa Barberini in Castel Gandolfo, with all endowments and appurtenances. This consignment must be effected within six months after the present treaty goes into effect.

In order to make one whole of the property sites on the north side of Janiculum Hill, belonging to the Sacred Congregation of Propaganda Fide and other ecclesiastical bodies which overlook the Vatican palaces, the State pledges the transfer to the Holy See or to other bodies designated later all real property of the State or of third parties existing in said zone. The real property belonging to said Congregation and other institutions, as well as other ones to be transferred, are indicated on the annexed plan.

Italy lastly transfers to the Holy See in full free property rights the convent edifices in Rome annexed to the basilica of the Holy Twelve Apostles, to the churches of St. Andrea della Valle and St. Charles dei Catinari, to be consigned free of all tenants within a year of the date the present treaty goes into effect.

ARTICLE FIFTEEN

Real estate designated in Article thirteen and in the first and second lines of Article fourteen, as well as the palaces Dataria, Cancelleria and Propaganda Fide in the Piazza di Spagna, and the Palace of the Holy Office and those adjacent thereto now used by the congregation of the Oriental Church in the Piazza Scossa Cavalli, and also the palace of the Vicariate and other edifices which the Holy See in the future deems necessary in order to arrange its departments, although forming a part of the territory of the Italian State, will enjoy the immunity recognized by international law to seats of diplomatic agents of foreign States.

The same immunity will be applied also regarding other churches and also in churches outside of Rome when there is celebrated in them, without being open to the public, ceremonies at which the Supreme Pontiff is present.

ARTICLE SIXTEEN

Real estate designated in the three preceding articles, as

well as that used for seats for the following pontifical institutes: namely, the Gregorian University, the Biblical Institute, the Oriental Institute, the Archeological Institute, the Russian Seminary, Lombard College, the two palaces of St. Apollinaris, as well as the house of spiritual retreat for the clergy at Sts. John and Paul, will never be subjected to liens or expropriations for cause of public utility without a preceding agreement with the Holy See. The State also will exempt it from taxes, whether ordinary or extraordinary, whether levied by the State or any other body.

The Holy See has the power to make whatever adjustment it believes suitable to all of the above real estate designated in the present article, and also in the three preceding articles, without need for authorization or consent on the part of Italian governmental, provincial or communal authorities, which can rely on the noble artistic traditions which the Catholic Church boasts.

ARTICLE SEVENTEEN

Contributions of whatever nature due to the Holy See by other central bodies of the Catholic Church or bodies directly managed by the Holy See, even outside of Rome, or to their dignitaries, employes and functionaries, even when not fixed, will be exempted in Italian territory, beginning January 1, 1929, from any tribute whatsoever both on the part of the State as well as any other body.

ARTICLE EIGHTEEN

The treasuries of art and science in the Vatican City and in the Lateran Palace will remain visible to scholars and

visitors, while full liberty will be reserved by the Holy See
to regulate when they shall be open to the public.

ARTICLE NINETEEN

Diplomats and envoys of the Holy See, diplomats and
envoys of foreign countries to the Holy See, dignitaries of
the church coming from abroad to the Vatican furnished
with a passport of the State of origin visaed by Papal
representatives abroad, can without any other formality
reach the Vatican through Italian territory. The same procedure will apply to those furnished with a regular pontifical
passport who go from the Vatican City abroad.

ARTICLE TWENTY

Merchandise from abroad coming to the Vatican City, or
outside the Vatican City for institutions or officers of the
Holy See, will always be admitted in any point within Italian confines or any port of the kingdom through Italian territory with full exemption of customs duties and intercom-
munal taxes.

ARTICLE TWENTY-ONE

Cardinals enjoy in Italy the same honors due princes of
the blood. Those resident in Rome, also those outside the
Vatican City, are citizens of the latter to all intents and purposes. During a vacancy in the pontifical See Italy provides in a special way that free transit and access of cardinals through Italian territory to the Vatican will not be
hindered, nor will any impediment or limit to personal liberty be placed on the same.

Italy in addition will take precautions that on the territory about the Vatican City acts will not be committed which

may disturb the neighborhood of the Vatican Conclave. Such regulations prevail also in Conclaves which may be held outside the Vatican City, also Councils presided over by the Holy Father or his legates, also as regards bishops called upon to participate therein.

ARTICLE TWENTY-TWO

On request of the Holy See, and also on delegation of power which can be given by the Holy See either in single cases or permanently, Italy will provide within her own territory for the punishment of crimes which are committed within the Vatican City, except when the author of the crime may have fled into Italian territory, in which case the procedure against him will be according to Italian laws. The Holy See will consign to the Italian State persons who have fled to the Vatican City charged with acts committed in Italian territory which may be considered criminal by the laws of both States. And analogous procedure will apply to persons charged with crime who flee to property declared immune in Article 15, unless those in charge of such property prefer to invite the Italian police to enter and arrest the fugitive.

ARTICLE TWENTY-THREE

For execution within the Kingdom of sentences emanating from tribunals of Vatican City, regulations of international law will be applied. Sentences and decrees issued by ecclesiastical authority and officially communicated to the civil authorities regarding ecclesiastical or religious persons, or concerning spiritual or disciplinary matters, will have at once full juridical efficiency for all civil purposes.

ARTICLE TWENTY-FOUR

The Holy See, in relation to the sovereignty due to it also in the international sphere, declares that it wishes to remain and will remain extraneous to all temporal disputes between States and to international congresses held for such objects, unless the contending parties make concordant appeal to its peaceful mission; at the same time reserving the right to exercise its moral and spiritual power.

In consequence of this declaration, Vatican City will always and in every case be considered neutral and inviolable territory.

ARTICLE TWENTY-FIVE

By special convention, signed jointly with the present treaty, and constituting the fourth annex to the same, and forming an integral part thereof, the liquidation of credits to the Holy See will be proceeded with.

ARTICLE TWENTY-SIX

The Holy See agrees that with the agreements signed today, adequate assurance is made for what is necessary for it for providing for due liberty and independence of the pastoral government of the diocese of Rome and the Catholic Church in Italy and the world, declares the Roman question definitely and irrevocably settled and therefore eliminated, and recognizes the Kingdom of Italy under the dynasty of the House of Savoy, with Rome the capital of the Italian State.

Italy in her turn recognizes the State of the Vatican City under the sovereignty of the Supreme Pontiff.

The law of the 15th of May, 1871, No. 214, is abrogated as well as any other decree contrary to the present treaty.

[N. B. This law is the so-called Law of Guarantees.]

Article Twenty-seven

The present treaty will be laid before the Supreme Pontiff and the King of Italy for ratification not later than four months from the date of signing, and will become effective on the act of the exchange of ratifications.

II

THE CONCORDAT

In the Name of the Most Holy Trinity:

Whereas, since the beginning of negotiations between the Holy See and Italy for resolution of the Roman question, the Holy See itself has proposed that a treaty relative to the said question should be accompanied as a necessary complement by a concordat for settling the conditions of religion and the church in Italy, and

Whereas, a treaty for solution of the Roman question has been concluded and signed today,

His Holiness, the Supreme Pontiff and His Majesty Victor Emmanuel III, King of Italy, have agreed to make a concordat and to this end have nominated the same plenipotentiaries delegated for stipulation of the treaty, that is to say, for His Holiness the Most Reverend Eminence Cardinal Pietro Gasparri, his Secretary of State, and for His Majesty Victor Emmanuel III, Signor Cavaliere Benito Mussolini, Premier and head of the Government, who, hav-

ing exchanged full credentials and found the same good
and in due form, have agreed to the following articles:

ARTICLE ONE

Italy, according to the terms of Article one of the
Treaty, assures to the Catholic Church free exercise of
spiritual power, free and public exercise of worship, as well
as jurisdiction in ecclesiastical matters, in conformity with
the regulations of the present concordat; where it is necessary accords to ecclesiastics the defense of its authority for
acts of their spiritual ministry. In consideration of the
sacred character of the Eternal City, Bishopric of the Supreme Pontiff and bourne of pilgrimages, the Italian Government will engage to prevent in Rome anything which
may conflict with the said character.

ARTICLE TWO

The Holy See communicates and corresponds freely
with bishops, the clergy and the whole Catholic world without any interference by the Italian Government. In the
same way, freely with their clergy and all the Faithful.

Both the Holy See and bishops may freely publish, also
affix to inside and external doors of edifices destined for
worship or offices of their ministry, instructions, ordinances,
pastoral letters, diocesan bulletins and other acts regarding
the spiritual government of the Faithful which they may
choose to issue within the province of their competence.
Such publications and notices, and generally all acts and
documents relative to the spiritual government of the Faithful, are not subject to taxes.

Such publications as regard the Holy See can be made

in any language. Those by bishops are made in Italian or Latin, but beside the Italian text the ecclesiastical authority may add a translation in other languages.

Ecclesiastical authorities may do so inside and at the doors of churches as well as edifices which are their property.

ARTICLE THREE

Theological students of the last two years of preparation in theology intended for the priesthood and novices in religious institutions may, on their request, postpone from year to year until the twenty-sixth year of age fulfillment of the obligations of military service.

Clerics ordained *in sacris* and members of Religious Orders who take vows are exempt from military service except in case of general mobilization. In such cases priests pass into the armed forces of the State, but maintain their Religious dress, so that they can practice among the troops their sacred ministry under the ecclesiastical jurisdiction of the military ordinary bishop. According to the terms they are preferentially attached to the health services.

At the same time, even if general mobilization is ordered, priests exercising full Divine rights are dispensed from the call to arms. Ordinaries, parish priests, parochial vicars or coadjutors, temporary vicars and priests permanently attached to rectories of churches open to worship are included in this category.

ARTICLE FOUR

Ecclesiastics and members of Religious Orders are exempt from the office of jurymen.

ARTICLE FIVE

No ecclesiastic can be employed or remain in the employment or offices of the Italian State or public bodies depending upon the same without *nulla osta* of the diocesan ordinary.

Revocation of *nulla osta* deprives the ecclesiastics of capacity to continue exercising employment or office taken up.

In any case apostate priests or those incurring censure cannot be employed in a teaching post or any office or employment in which they have immediate contact with the public.

[N. B. *Nulla osta* means "nothing hinders."]

ARTICLE SIX

Stipends and other emoluments enjoyed by ecclesiastics on account of their office are exempt from charges and liens in the same way as stipends and salaries of State employes.

ARTICLE SEVEN

Ecclesiastics cannot be requested by magistrates or other authorities to give information regarding persons or matters that have come to their knowledge through the exercise of their sacred ministry.

ARTICLE EIGHT

In the case of the sending of an ecclesiastic or a member of a Religious Order before a penal magistrate for crime, the King's procurator must relate the proceedings thereof to the ordinary of the diocese in whose territory he exercises jurisdiction, and must immediately transmit to the office of the ordinary the preliminary decision thereon and, if issued, the final sentence, both of the court of first instance and the court of appeal.

In the case of arrest, the ecclesiastic or member of a Religious Order is treated with the respect due to his state and hierarchic degree. In case of the sentence of an ecclesiastic or member of an ecclesiastical order, punishment is to be, if possible, undergone in places separate from those designated for laymen, unless a competent ordinary has reduced the prisoner to a lay state.

Article Nine

As a general rule edifices open for worship are exempt from confiscation or occupation.

When for grave public necessity it becomes necessary to occupy an edifice open to worship, the authority proceeding with the occupation must make previous arrangements with the ordinary, unless reasons of absolute urgency are opposed thereto. In this case the occupying authority must immediately inform the ordinary.

Except in cases of urgent necessity the public force cannot enter for the exercise of its functions edifices open to worship without previous notice to the ecclesiastical authorities.

Article Ten

For no reason is it permitted to proceed with the demolition of edifices open to worship except by previous agreement with competent ecclesiastical authorities.

Article Eleven

The State recognizes the holidays established by the Church, which are: All Sundays, New Year's Day, Epiphany, St. Joseph's Day (March 19), Ascension Day, Corpus Christi, the Feast of the Apostles Sts. Peter and Paul (June 29), the Assumption of the Blessed Virgin Mary (August 15), All Saints' Day, the Feast of the Immaculate Conception (December 8) and Christmas Day.

Article Twelve

On Sundays and fixed Church holidays, where there is a chapter, the celebrant of high mass will sing according to the liturgy a prayer for the prosperity of the King of Italy and the Italian State.

Article Thirteen

The Italian Government will communicate to the Holy See a full list of the ecclesiastical personnel regularly attached to its service for spiritual assistance with the military forces of the State, as soon as same is approved according to law.

The choice of ecclesiastics charged with the high direction of the service of spiritual assistance—military ordinary, vicar and inspectors—is made confidentially by the Holy See to the Italian Government. Whenever the Italian Government has reasons for opposing such choice, it will communicate the same to the Holy See, which will proceed to another choice.

The military ordinary will have the rank of archbishop.

The nomination of military chaplains is made by competent authorities of the Italian State on choice of the military ordinary.

ARTICLE FOURTEEN

The Italian aeronautical, terrestrial and naval troops shall enjoy in regard to religious duties the privileges and exemptions permitted by Canon Law.

Military chaplains have, as regards said troops, parochial stipends. They exercise a sacred ministry under the jurisdiction of the military ordinary, assisted by his own curia.

The Military Ordinary has jurisdiction also over the religious personnel, male or female, attached to the military hospitals.

ARTICLE FIFTEEN

The ordinary military Archbishop is attached to a chapter of the Church of the Pantheon in Rome, constituting with it the clergy charged with religious service at the said basilica.

Such clergy are authorized to attend all religious functions, even outside of Rome, which in conformity with canonical regulations, may be requested by the State or the Royal Household.

The Holy See agrees to confer on all canons forming the chapter of the Church of the Pantheon the dignity of Apostolic Prothonotaries *ad instar durante munere*. The nomination of each of them will be made by the Cardinal Vicar of Rome after presentation by His Majesty the King of Italy, and following confidential indication of the candidates.

The Holy See reserves the right to transfer the Deaconry to another church.

14819

The high contracting parties will proceed by agreement through the operation of mixed commissions to a revision of the diocesan limits in order to make them correspond with the provinces of each State.

It is understood that the Holy See will create a Diocese of Zara; that no part of the territory subject to the sovereignty of the Kingdom of Italy will depend upon a bishop whose territory is subject to the sovereignty of another State; and no diocese of the Kingdom of Italy will include territorial zones subject to the sovereignty of another State.

The same principle will be observed for all parishes existing or to be created in territories near each State.

Modifications which, after the agreement heretofore outlined, may be made to diocesan limits, will be arranged by the Holy See in agreement with the Italian Government and in observance of the principles laid down, except for small rectifications of territory required for spiritual needs.

ARTICLE SEVENTEEN

The reduction of the number of dioceses to result from the application of the preceding article will be carried into effect gradually as the dioceses become vacant.

It is understood that the reduction will not imply suppression of titles within the dioceses or of chapters which will be maintained, but that the dioceses will be regrouped in such a manner that the chief towns of the same will correspond with those of the provinces.

The aforesaid reductions will leave untouched all of the present economic reserves of the dioceses and other ecclesiastical bodies existing within the same, including the sums now paid by the Italian State.

ARTICLE EIGHTEEN

Owing to the necessity, by disposition of ecclesiastical authority, of uniting several parishes in a temporary or definite way, either by intrusting them to one parish priest assisted by one or more vice parish priests, or by uniting several priests into one presbytery, the State shall maintain unchanged the economic allowance due these parishes.

ARTICLE NINETEEN

The choice of archbishops and bishops belongs to the Holy See. Before an archbishop, bishop or coadjutor with the right of succession is nominated, the Holy See shall communicate the name of the chosen person to the Italian Government, in order to be sure that the Government has no objections of a political nature against such person. The formalities to this effect shall be carried out with all possible haste and with the greatest discretion, so that secrecy about the chosen candidate shall be maintained until he is formally nominated.

ARTICLE TWENTY

All bishops, before their installation in their respective dioceses, shall take an oath at the hands of the Premier under the following formula:

"Before God and on the Holy Gospels I swear and promise to respect and cause my clergy to respect the King and Government as they are established under the constitutional laws of the State. I furthermore swear and promise not to participate in any agreement or attend any council which would be injurious to the Italian State, or to the public peace, and not to permit my clergy any such participation. Being mindful only of the welfare and interest of the Italian State, I will endeavor to avoid anything which might menace them."

ARTICLE TWENTY-ONE

The choice of persons for ecclesiastical benefices belongs to the ecclesiastical authority. The appointment of such persons shall be communicated confidentially to the Italian Government by the proper church authorities. Appointments cannot be approved until thirty days have elapsed since such communication. In the meantime the Italian Government, if it has any objection to an appointment, may manifest it confidentially to the ecclesiastical authority which, in the event a discrepancy of views persists, shall submit the case to the Holy See.

Should serious objections against the exercise of an ecclesiastical benefice by a priest arise, the Italian Government shall communicate such objections to the bishop, who, by agreement with the Government, shall take appropriate measures within three months. In the event of a controversy between the bishop and the Government, the Holy See shall refer the solution to two ecclesiastics of its own choice, who, by agreement with two delegates from the Italian Government, shall make a final decision.

ARTICLE TWENTY-TWO

Ecclesiastics who are not Italian citizens cannot be made the holders of benefices existing in Italy. Bishops and parish priests must speak Italian. If necessary they must have coadjutors who, besides Italian, must understand and speak also the local language, for the purpose of giving religious assistance in the language of the Faithful in accordance with the rules of the church.

Article Twenty-three

The provisions of Articles sixteen, seventeen, nineteen, twenty, twenty-one and twenty-two are not to be applied to Rome and its suburban dioceses.

It is agreed that, in the event the Holy See reorganizes such dioceses, allowances now paid by the Italian Government to parishes or other ecclesiastical institutions shall remain unchanged.

Article Twenty-four

The *exequatur* and the royal *placet,* or any other royal appointment in the matter of ecclesiastical benefices and offices, are abolished throughout Italy except the exemptions set by Article twenty-nine, "seventh."

Article Twenty-five

The Italian State renounces the royal prerogatives concerning major and minor ecclesiastical benefices. The right exercised by the State of using the allowances during the vacancy of ecclesiastical benefices is abolished.

Article Twenty-six

Appointment of those who shall enjoy major or minor benefices, or those who temporarily represent a vacant see or benefice, shall be effective from the date on which the appointment is communicated officially to the Italian Government. The administration and the use of income during such vacancy are regulated by the rule of canon law. In case of bad management, the Italian State, after agreement with the ecclesiastical authorities, can seize the income, turning it over to the person in charge or, in the latter's absence, to the institution.

ARTICLE TWENTY-SEVEN

The basilicas and Holy House at Loreto, St. Francis at Assisi, St. Anthony at Padua, together with the buildings and institutions annexed thereto, except those having merely a lay character, shall be ceded to the Holy See, and their administration shall freely belong to the Holy See. All institutions of any sort which are conducted by the Holy See in Italy, together with missionary colleges, shall likewise be free from any interference from the Italian Government. Purchases of property by moral bodies shall, however, be subject to Italian laws. The property and title of the foregoing basilicas shall be defined by mixed commissions, who shall take due account of the rights of third parties or the endowments which are necessary to the foregoing lay institutions. Ecclesiastical administration shall replace civil administration in churches in which the latter administration is existing.

ARTICLE TWENTY-EIGHT

In order to appease the conscience of those who, under Italian law, own ecclesiastical property, the Holy See grants full recognition to the title of such property. The Holy See will advise bishops to this effect.

ARTICLE TWENTY-NINE

The Italian State shall revise its legislation in so far

as ecclesiastical matters are concerned in order to make it conform to the aspirations inspiring both the treaty and the concordat. The high contracting parties agree forthwith as follows:

First, to leaving unchanged the juridical status of ecclesiastical bodies hitherto recognized by Italian laws (namely the Holy See, its dioceses, chapters, seminaries, parishes and so forth). Such status shall be extended to churches open to worship which hitherto have not been in possession of it, including those formerly belonging to ecclesiastical bodies which were suppressed. Except for what is provided in Article 27, the boards of administrators, wherever they may exist and whatever their denomination, even if composed of a majority or totally of laymen, shall not interfere with services of worship, while appointment of such boards shall be made in agreement with ecclesiastical authorities.

Second, the juridical status shall be recognized of religious associations with or without vows which are approved by the Holy See, which have their mother house in Italy which are represented, *de jure* or *de facto*, by persons having Italian citizenship and who live in Italy. The juridical status also is recognized of Italian Religious provinces within the boundaries of the Italian State and its colonial possessions, also of associations having their mother house abroad, provided the same conditions are implied, also of Religious houses, when the particular rules of each Order attribute to them the capacity of buying or owning, also of the headquarters of Religious Orders, also of provinces of foreign religious associations. Associations and Religious houses already enjoying juridical status will maintain it.

Third, confraternities the main purpose of which is to worship shall not be subject to further alteration of their aims and purposes, and they shall depend upon ecclesiastical authorities in so far as their functioning and administration are concerned.

Fourth, the existence of religious foundations of any sort is permitted, provided that it is manifest that they respond to the religious need of the population and that there is no financial obligation on the part of the State. The above provision also applies to existing foundations.

Fifth, one half of the membership of boards of civil administrators of ecclesiastical estates formed after such estates were seized by the State shall be composed of members designated by ecclesiastical authorities. The same provision applies to religious funds in new provinces.

Sixth, acts done hitherto by ecclesiastical and religious bodies without complying with civil laws may be recognized and regularized by the Italian State upon demand of the bishop to be submitted within three months of the date upon which the present concordat becomes operative.

Seventh, the Italian State surrenders jurisdiction over the palatine clergy throughout Italy, except the clergy attached to the Church of St. Veronica of the Handkerchief at Turin, the church at Superga, the Church of the Sudario at Rome, and chapels annexed to the royal palaces or the residences of members of the royal family. A special commission shall attend to assigning adequate endowment to each palatine church or basilica under the criteria set for churches in Article twenty-seven.

Eighth, leaving unchanged the taxation facilities already enjoyed by ecclesiastical bodies under existing Italian laws, the purpose of worship or religion is placed on the same footing as the purpose of benevolence or culture insofar as taxation is concerned. The extra tax of thirty per cent imposed by the law of August 15, 1867, the so-called contribution taxes provided by the laws of July 7, 1866, and August 15, 1867, and the tax on the transfer of ecclesiastical property imposed by the royal decree of December, 1923, are abolished. Any special tax on church property is excluded in the future. Clergymen shall be exempted from taxation insofar as the exercise of their sacerdotal ministry is concerned, or any other tax of the kind.

Ninth, the use of religious garb by laymen, or by clergymen who are prohibited from wearing it by definite order of the proper ecclesiastical authorities—an order which must be communicated to the Italian Government—is forbidden and punished with the same penalties which are meted to those who illicitly wear the military uniform.

Article Thirty

Ordinary and extraordinary administration of any property belonging to any ecclesiastical institute or religious association is carried out under the supervision and control of the proper church authorities, and any interference by the Italian State is excluded.

The Italian State, until it is established otherwise through new accords, shall continue making up inadequacy in incomes of vacant ecclesiastical benefits through allowances in measure not inferior to that granted by present laws. Therefore, the management of such benefits—so far as acts and contracts beyond simple administration are concerned—shall be effected with the intervention of the Italian

State. Income of Rome suburban dioceses and income of chapters and parishes in Rome are not subject to the aforesaid intervention. The amount of income of such dioceses, chapters and parishes shall be announced yearly by bishops, dioceses and the Cardinal Vicar of Rome in order that they may get the extra allowance provided under the present laws.

ARTICLE THIRTY-ONE

The creation of new ecclesiastical bodies or religious associations shall be made by ecclesiastical authority in accordance with the rules of canon law and recognition of their juridical status, so far as civil effects are concerned, shall be made by civil authorities.

ARTICLE THIRTY-TWO

Recognition and authorizations provided in the present concordat and treaty shall occur through rules set by civil laws which shall be made to conform to provisions of the treaty and concordat.

ARTICLE THIRTY-THREE

Ownership of the Catacombs existing in Rome and in other places in Italy shall be ceded to the Holy See which undertakes to guard, keep up and preserve them. Therefore, the Holy See after complying with the laws of the State and respecting the eventual rights of third parties is empowered to proceed to the necessary excavations and to remove the holy bodies.

ARTICLE THIRTY-FOUR

The Italian State, wishing to reinvest the institution of marriage, which is the basis of the family, with the dignity conformable to the Catholic traditions of its people, recognizes the Sacrament of Matrimony performed according to canon law as fully effective in civil law. Notices of such marriages will be made both in the parish church and in the town or city hall. Immediately after the celebration of such marriage, the parish priest will explain to those he has married the civil effect of matrimony, reading the articles of the civil code regarding the rights and duties of spouses and will prepare the marriage certificate, a copy of which he will send within five days to the commune in order that it may be copied into the registers by the civil authorities.

Cases concerning nullity of marriage and dispensation from marriage by reason of nonconsummation, are reserved for ecclesiastical tribunals and departments.

Decrees and respective sentences here, when they become final, will be brought before the supreme tribunal of Segnatura, which will decide if the rules of canon law regarding jurisdiction of the court, citation and proper appearance or non-appearance of the parties concerned have been respected.

Such decrees and final sentences with the decisions of the supreme court of Segnatura will be transmitted to the appeal court having jurisdiction over the case, which by means of an order issued in council will render the same executive for all civil purposes, and will order that they be inscribed on the civil registers of the State alongside the record of the marriage act.

As regards cases of personal separation, the Holy See agrees that the same be judged by the civil judicial authority.

ARTICLE THIRTY-FIVE

For middle schools maintained by ecclesiastical or religious bodies, the institution of State examination remains unchanged with equal opportunities for candidates of government and religious institutions.

ARTICLE THIRTY-SIX

Italy considers the teaching of Christian Doctrine according to the forms received from Catholic tradition as the foundation and crown of public education. Therefore Italy consents that the religious teaching now imparted in the elementary schools be further developed in the secondary schools according to a program to be agreed upon between the Holy See and the State.

Such instruction will be given by masters, professors, priests and members of religious orders approved by ecclesiastical authorities and in subsidiary form by lay masters and professors furnished with proper certificates of capacity issued by the diocesan ordinary.

Revocation of the certificate by the ordinary immediately deprives the teacher of authority to instruct. Only textbooks approved by the ecclesiastical authorities will be used in the public schools for such religious teaching.

ARTICLE THIRTY-SEVEN

Directors of State associations for physical education and preliminary instruction of "Avanguardisti" and "Balilla," in order to render possible religious teaching and assistance for the youth in their charge, will arrange so that the schedule will not prevent fulfillment of religious duties by boys on Sundays and fixed religious holidays.

Similarly directors of public schools will arrange as regards assemblies of scholars on holidays.

ARTICLE THIRTY-EIGHT

Professors of the Catholic University of the Sacred Heart and the dependent Institute of Mary the Immaculate are subordinated to *nulla osta* by order of the Holy See to insure that no exception will be able to be taken from a moral or religious point of view.

ARTICLE THIRTY-NINE

Universities, major and minor seminaries, whether diocesan, inter-diocesan or local, academies, colleges and other Catholic institutes for the formation and culture of ecclesiastics will continue to depend solely upon the Holy See without any interference on the part of scholastic authorities of the Kingdom.

ARTICLE FORTY

Degrees in sacred theology issued by faculties and approved by the Holy See will be recognized by the Italian State.

Similarly diplomas will be recognized which are conferred in schools of paleography, the archive of science and documentary diplomacy existing in the library and the archives of the Vatican City.

ARTICLE FORTY-ONE

Italy will authorize for use in the kingdom and colonies of pontifical knightly honors, by means of registration of the patent nomination to be made effective by presentation of the patent and written request of the interested party.

Article Forty-two

Italy will admit recognition by royal decree of noble titles conferred by the Supreme Pontiff even after 1870 and also those to be conferred in the future. In cases to be determined such recognition will not be subject to an initial payment of tax.

Article Forty-three

The Italian State recognizes organizations dependent on "Azione Cattolica Italiana," inasmuch as they, as the Holy See has declared, exercise activity outside all political parties and are under the immediate direction of the hierarchy of the church for diffusion and propaganda of Catholic principles. The Holy See takes the present occasion of the stipulation of this concordat to renew to all ecclesiastics and members of religious orders in Italy the prohibition against joining or taking part in any political party.

Article Forty-four

If in the future any difficulty should arise on the interpretation of the present concordat, the Holy See and Italy will proceed equably to an amicable solution.

Article Forty-five

The present concordat will be effective on the exchange of ratification contemporaneously with the treaty stipulated between the high contracting parties eliminating the Roman Question. With the becoming effective of the present Concordat, all regulations deriving from concordats made by former Italian States will cease to have effect. Austrian laws, laws and regulations, decrees and ordinances of the

Italian State at present effective, are abrogated when the present Concordat becomes effective, insofar as they are in opposition to the terms of this Concordat.

In order to carry into effect the present Concordat, there will be nominated immediately after the signing thereof, a commission composed of persons chosen by both parties.

III
FINANCIAL CONVENTION

ARTICLE ONE

Italy undertakes to pay upon the exchange of ratifications of the treaty, to the Holy See the sum of 750,000,000 Italian lire and to hand at the same time to the Holy See Italian five per cent negotiable consolidated bonds—with coupons falling due on June 30 next—to the nominal value of 1,000,000,000 Italian lire.

ARTICLE TWO

The Holy See declares that it accepts the above as a definite settlement of its financial relations with Italy depending upon the events of 1870.

ARTICLE THREE

All deeds to be executed for the effectuation of the treaty, this convention and the Concordat shall be exempt from all taxes.

Appendix B

An Historic Document

Translated from the *Osservatore Romano*, of
February 12-13, 1929

IN the Hall of the Popes of the Apostolic Lateran Palace, at twelve o'clock noon, a treaty was signed between the Holy See and Italy, whereby the "Roman Question" was settled, a Concordat to regulate the religious status of the Church in Italy was reached, and a definite financial agreement was juridically concluded: the chief signers thereto being His Eminence, the Most Reverend Pietro Cardinal Gasparri, Secretary of State to His Holiness, His Excellency, Signor Cavaliere Benito Mussolini, Prime Minister and Head of the Italian Government. The solemn pact was signed in the presence of Monsignor Francesco Borgongini Duca, Secretary of the Sacred Congregation of Extraor-

NOTE: This is published as a historic document. It appeared in the original in the *Osservatore Romano* the day after the Treaty and Concordat were signed. It is by Count dalla Torre, and was translated by Gabriel A. Zema, S.J.

dinary Ecclesiastical Affairs; Monsignor Giuseppe Piz-
zardo, Assistant Secretary of State, and the Hon. Professor
and Doctor of Laws, Francesco Pacelli, Jurisconsult of the
Holy See. Representing Italy were their Excellencies Signor Alfredo Rocco, Minister of Seals; Signor Dino Grandi,
Under-secretary of the Ministry of Foreign Affairs, and
Signor Francesco Giunta, Secretary of the Presidency of
the Council.

It was on the feast of Our Lady of Lourdes, merciful
Protectress of the Papacy, on the feast of her whose special
prerogative of the Immaculate Conception was proclaimed
as a dogma to the whole world in the Cathedral of the
Popes, that the solemn pact between Italy and the Holy
See, between Church and State, was signed.

"THE SOLEMN HOUR"

I

Terms of the Roman Question

THE significance of the Roman Question has been ac-
curately defined in a letter by Pope Leo XIII concerning the government of the Church, addressed to the Secretary of State, Cardinal Mariano Rampolla, June 15, 1887:

The authority of the Supreme Pontiff, instituted by Jesus Christ
and conferred upon St. Peter, and through him to us, his legitimate
successors, the Roman Pontiffs, is destined to perpetuate in the world
to its very end the redemptive work of the Son of God. This power
has been enriched by the most noble prerogatives, endowed with
exalted powers of its own, and juridical powers as well, such as are
required in the government of a true and perfect society. Hence
that authority by its very nature and by the express will of the
Divine Founder of the Church cannot be subject to any earthly

power whatever, but must actually enjoy the most ample liberty in order to carry on its sacred ministry.

For since the well-being of the entire Church depends upon this supreme power and upon the free exercise thereof, it was of the greatest importance that its original liberty and independence should be assured, guaranteed and defended throughout the ages in the person of him in whom it was invested.

. . . It must be carefully borne in mind, however, that the reason for the liberty and independence of the Papacy in the exercise of its Apostolic ministry has a greater value and a peculiarly distinctive force when applied to Rome, the natural residence of the Supreme Pontiffs, the center of the life of the Church and the capital of the Catholic world.

In Rome, where the Pontiff ordinarily resides, the center whence he directs, teaches, and commands; so that all the Faithful may pay him dutiful respect from every part of the world and render him obedience with security and trust;—it is in Rome that it is especially necessary that he be in such status of independence that not only shall his liberty be not in the least curtailed by anyone, but that none be there to violate it.

Calling to mind the historical background of the civil supremacy of the Church, providentially sustained over the upheaval of medieval empires and kingdoms and uninterruptedly preserved in spite of the stormy vicissitudes of a thousand years, a shield of the Holy See and the mainstay of Italian culture, Pope Leo XIII's letter vindicated the reestablishment of this civil sovereignty independent of any "different form (of government) and (territorial) extension"; for it is the only expression and safeguard of real visible sovereignty according to the precepts of international law.

Such policy fully shows that this juridical guaranty has always been looked upon as the means to a spiritual end of the free and independent government of the Church; that it was, therefore, necessary for the influence of religion that it be claimed not for itself, not in behalf of any temporal dominion whatever, but only to vindicate inviolable rights and undeniable duties associated with the God-given ministry of the Papacy.

"They venture to assert," declared Leo XIII in an allocution to Cardinal Alimonda and to the Italian priests who had journeyed as pilgrims to Rome, "that the vindication of the Pontiff's rights is dictated by a spirit of ambition and worldly grandeur! . . . Our aim scales far loftier heights than that—it is the cause of our very liberty and independence that we espouse."

It was an attitude of mind shared by all the Popes, from Leo down to Pius XI. In his first Encyclical Pius XI ("Ubi Arcano Dei") saw and placed the same Roman Question in that great framework of world affairs which he made a matter of deep study and concern. He studied moral evils and proposed those remedies which could only be administered to mankind by religion and the Church, after they had been restored to their ancient place of honor.

"By the violation of the guarantees providentially secured to the liberty of the Roman Pontiff," declared the Pope, "an abnormal situation has been brought about that is a source of grave and permanent disturbance of the conscience of Catholics throughout the world. . . . We protest in defence of the rights and dignity of the Apostolic See not indeed through a spirit of vain and worldly ambition, which should indeed be unworthy of us, but purely in behalf of conscience."

Thus every objection was answered. Every subtle

equivocation was answered by which (Masonic) sects tried to misrepresent the Roman Question as a "political question" before Italians and before all peoples—or tried to place the protests and representations of the Holy See on the same level as the protests of powerless princes in times past against the birth of a new political unity and the juridical succession of a new Italian State.

Truth was nevertheless unyielding. The Roman Question was purely a religious question which the Pope, the Vicar of Christ, the Head of the Church and not merely the Sovereign of the Papal States, declared to be unsolved.

When there was question, therefore, in 1870 of the ancient and traditional guarantee of the Pope's free and independent pastoral office and of his liberty and independence, an altogether essential and inviolable right existed— a right that can never be confused with nor measured by the material element of the guarantee itself. . . . The Supreme Pontiff himself is not an arbiter of that right, because it is inherent in the Divine constitution of the Church. But the means of establishing that guarantee—its extent and conditions—of this the Pope is the sole arbiter: he alone is the judge.

II

The Precedents of Sixty Years

These principles, these fixed posts of historical groundwork of sixty years remained unchanged from the pontificate of Pius IX to that of Pius XI. They can be traced logically and directly to the great question which in its uninterrupted existence amongst countless vicissitudes and periodical vindications of its claims, does not change. It does not change when its claims are boldly denied; it does not change in spite of studied trickery to drag it from its rightful juridical status, to see it in an unnatural connotation, and to strip it of its spiritual characteristics, moral and juridical. That question does not change as long as the Popes, concerned only for the religious interests of the people, and more than ever gravely threatened by disturbances in the field of ideas by social and political upheavals and actual war—show themselves ready to consider any solution that will remedy the losses and damages to the Church and to society as long as it will safeguard the integrity of the Church's principles and the inviolability of her rights.

Leo XIII

The name of Leo XIII becomes grander, more exalted and auspicious at this moment, when fairness and peace are realized. Leo XIII was not spared by the (Masonic) sects, as Pius IX had not been spared before him. He appeared to be even a greater target of abuse than Pius. Not because he asserted his relentless resistance to them, but rather because of the indomitable genius with which, at this crisis as at all others, he unmasked every sworn doctrinaire, exposed all ingenious trickery and presented his own clear, logical and irrefutable position before the consciousness of the people. For his defence was not only the buckler of sound reason, but also the breastplate of unassailable argument that appealed to those who loved truth and goodness.

Pope Leo XIII's success in putting the Roman Question

on the high road of settlement won greater opposition for him. Indeed he was a special object of attack because he strenuously pleaded for the need of prompt solution. The venerable Pontiff loved the Italian people and the land of his birth with the deepest love of father, pastor, and we may say even, of poet and artist, against all the attacks and treacheries of his adversaries who were ever quick to impede every project that he sought to carry out. And yet, he was ready to come to terms if, as he was wont to say, Italy placed her trust in the Church. If no settlement was reached it was not because his desire of peace was less keen even against the overreaching opposition of the (Masonic) sects who managed to dominate the too vacillating wills of certain Italian statesmen.

It was a dream of peace as yet to be realized when the white smoke rose from the Vatican hill, announcing Giuseppe Sarto as the gloriously reigning Pontiff, Pope Pius X.

Pius X

But the unfriendly hold on affairs of State went on as usual and the attitude became even more unfriendly because of the meekness of Pius X. The peace-loving soul of the saintly Pontiff sought every friendly approach that was possible and every means of condescension consonant with charity and justice. There was talk then only of "temporal power," breaking down at a single stroke all previous agreements to the contrary and giving these two words an erroneous significance with the hope of destroying the very terms of the question. In place of religious liberty was postulated ambition of temporal rule; instead of a solemn vindication of a spiritual sovereignty, there was question only of a grasping desire of material gain in the minds of the foes of *Pio Decimo*.

With that characteristic firmness that naturally manifested itself whenever the dignity and the rights of the Church were questioned he stayed every advance of her foes. He made it a point to speak clearly at all times and to insist on the Roman Question, on the prerogatives of the Holy See and on the liberty and independence of the Pope, without so much as mentioning the so-called "temporal power";—and whenever reference to it had to be made it was merely "civil sovereignty," and even those terms were limited by the qualifying condition that should forestall a divided opinion even amongst Catholics. He had in mind at all times the claims of the Pope, and nothing but those fair and inviolable claims.

Prima lo spirituale—His spiritual rights were of first importance, His Holiness averred, and he gave eloquent proof of his chagrin to the Italians, showing that the uncompromising *non expedit* was based "on very grave reasons intended for the supreme good of society which must at all costs be saved from disaster." He made that same policy clear to the Bishops who would "recognize their sacred mission for the good of souls and the supreme interests of their churches." In 1911 this paper voiced the opinion that there should be no question about the "temporal power" *in se* and *per se* but question only of guarantees, and of the sovereign rights of the Holy See which was therefore disposed to consider any feasible and legitimate parley looking towards an adequate solution of the problem. The policy of "Catholic Action" made known in Venice in 1913 was clearly that Italian Catholics should claim again the liberty and independence of the Pope and that they should persuade themselves that because of the Church's infallible teaching the protection and the liberty of their religion would be thereby assured, and that their conscience would no longer be fettered by unjust laws. This was their clear duty, since it is for the Holy See alone to establish the norm of a fair treaty or the limits of a satisfactory Concordat. When at the time of the "Social Week" in Milan of the same year the slogan of the "civil liberty of Catholics" was raised, it augured well even then that peace between Church and State and the adequate solution of a problem so much sought for, and that involved such opposite views, could be reached only through the constitutional will of the greater number.

BENEDICT XV

Rumors, hopes, suggestions, when the fury of the war was at its height, hinting that in the event of victory for the Central Powers "temporal power" should be restored, yielded to no less an authority than Cardinal Gasparri, Benedict XV's Secretary of State, faithful interpreter of his policy as Pope and as Sovereign, who spoke in the following words in the *Stimmen der Zeit* for September, 1916:

Faithful to its policy of neutrality the Holy See has no intention of causing embarrassment to the Government in any way and it places its confidence in God, awaiting the dispositions of His providence for a systematic and satisfactory adjustment of its affairs. Its reliance is not on foreign arms, but upon the triumph of justice which it believes the Italian people will mete out with an increased appreciation of the value to its own interests as well.

No one realized then that such significant and memorable words sowed in a soil as yet untilled were to yield a harvest of friendly interest in the field of politics and of law of a more maturely educated Italy, and that we were today to see the fruitful yielding of the seed sown so far back. At any rate as we look back it is clear that those words uttered in the din of battle and enunciated again in the calm of peace once more gave expression to a great prinple involved in the question. "Not from foreign armies" was the keynote of campaign, and that meant "not through foreign Governments." The Roman Question was not an international question in the sense of outside interference, but a morally supra-national question that was closely linked to the religious interests of all Christian peoples; a question, moreover, that had a legal force between the Italian State and the Holy See just as in the case of the original entanglement. This paper declared even as late as 1927: "We do not invoke foreign powers or international tribunals. Upon foreign Powers it will devolve only to take note of such formulae as usage may dictate, in whatever accord Italy may make with the Holy See."

If Pius X had thus far cleared the field of controversy of those stubborn and underhand insinuations implied in the phrase "temporal power," the work of Benedict XV stands out in the fact that he refuted and overcame such international jealousies as were aroused by the (Masonic) sects under the pretext of setting the Italian conscience at ease and safeguarding the interests of the Italian State. In reality, however, they were attacking the loyalty and the honor of the people and the Government as well; for they should have rather pointed out the duty of settling a long-drawn-out conflict. This position which was so aptly taken with regard to the problem met with its logical development in the action taken by the same Pontiff at the visit of the Catholic Sovereigns to Rome.

In behalf of peace and only because this gift of God is one of the greatest blessings for mankind, only in order to mitigate the consequences of the war and to settle all differences arising amongst dissatisfied parties, to bind the nations into closer bonds of amity and to restore and quicken the spirit of brotherhood in the hearts of men;— it was especially for such motives as these that Benedict XV issued the encyclical "Pacem Dei Munus," "in order to relax the strictness of those conditions" which were required in such cases by "the Holy See, shorn of its civil supremacy." Here again the same "grave reasons"—in the spiritual and moral order—which governed the reservations and protests of the Popes, asked for an exception, a derogation from the rule. Here again, if the "Roman Question" had been merely a "political question" and had been defended merely on a material basis, this new instance of the relaxation would never have occurred.

Pius XI

Finally, when on February 6, 1922, Pope Pius XI appeared unexpectedly on the Loggia of St. Peter's to bless Rome, Italy and the world, that indubitable omen of reconciliation became a new harbinger of hope in every heart. Everyone felt that the blessing of Pius XI brought with it a vague but not less real portent that the long and auspicious flight of Italian and world peace had been directed Romewards and was eventually to alight upon that Basilica,

upon that residence of the Popes and of the soul of the
Church as the terminus of its sojourn,—the long-sighed-for
goal, the dearly cherished boon of the prayers of Catholics
the world over.

For the current avowal that the rights of the Church
and of the Holy See were intact, even if it silenced for a
time the insolent and disrespectful comment concerning the
Holy Father's blessing from the Loggia of St. Peter's, in
no way lessened the importance of the mystical bond, at
once generous and fatherly, with which the newly elected
Pontiff was drawing his children far and near to himself, especially those nearest to him,—a bond that was a source of
encouragement and high hope.

As a matter of fact, a few months later, in the Encyclical of December 23, 1922, speaking of the mysterious and
solemn hour of well-omened peace, the fatherly heart of the
Pope and Primate of Italy thus expressed itself:

Italy has had and will have nothing to fear from the Holy
See. The Pope, whoever he will be, will always repeat: "I think
thoughts of peace and not of affliction"; thoughts, therefore, of true
peace that is inseparable from justice . . . It is for God to draw
this hour unto us and to give its glad tidings. For men who are
wise and of good will may that hour sound not in vain. It will be
among the most solemn and auspicious hours for the restoration of
the reign of Christ and for the peace of Italy and of the world.

III

Negotiations

And that hour has struck. Its sound was carried by the
echo of Providence into the consciousness of him who,
steering through the arduous course of power and responsi-

bility, acknowledged and stabilized the traditions of the Italians. He recognized that their religious instincts were of first importance to the civic and social greatness of Italy and that in the Catholic Church and in the person of the Roman Pontiff must be recognized its most influential guide and its safest teacher.

It is now two years since Signor Mussolini first intimated his willingness to the Holy Father to solve the Roman Question. Prompted by his own keen appreciation of the matter and inspired by the well-known sentiments of his predecessors, the Pope secured the approval of every Cardinal. The unanimous consent of the Sacred College to the head of the Italian government was that there would be need of private and confidential preliminary discussion of the matter. But even then it was stipulated that these tentative negotiations and conclusions on the Roman Question must proceed from and be defined in conjunction with the terms of a Concordat between the Church and the State and the adjustment of the Church's religious status in Italy. No nobler manner of procedure, the Holy Father felt, could be more worthy of a Father dealing with his children and his generous desire was heartily complied with.

Under these happy auspices the difficult task was undertaken and the settlement of this two-sided and very intricate problem was reached after some two hundred meetings. These meetings represented deep study and the discussion of the problem's many-sided aspects. It was a work of love and diligent effort and if one note more than another may be stressed, it is that of mutual good will and understanding of both State and Church.

The long-sought-for solution was reached on the following basis . . . The Italian State subscribes to a treaty that abrogates the Law of Guarantees; she recognizes the principle of an effective and full power and the sovereign jurisdiction of the Supreme Pontiff over a determined territory, the City of the Vatican; she also assigns a sum of money in recompense for ancient provinces, pontifical properties and losses incurred by ecclesiastical units. She stipulates a Concordat upon the agreements between the Church and the Italian State. The Holy See declares the Roman Question as settled and it recognizes among the constitutive and formative elements of that settlement, the Kingdom of Italy.

And here the pen might well write down its *Nunc dimittis*. In the sight of so noble a deed it could not do better than rewrite the famous epitaph: *Nullum par elogium*. But there is no question of this. Eulogy is matter only for history,—history that will transmit for all time the memory of a peace that was reached between two Powers whose conflict had too long been injurious to religion and to culture, the two primary sources of life and social order, and it will acknowledge the greatness of soul of a Pontiff, the wisdom of a Monarch, the wise and fruitful labors of the two principal representatives vested with extraordinary powers.

It will be for us to tell of the occasion of the solemn ratification of the pacts—a less exalted, but none the less a useful and praiseworthy service—and to point out the principal lines of agreement in behalf of public opinion. For public opinion is after all not satisfied with flashes of enthusiasm nor is it formed by intuitive knowledge, but should be grounded on solid convictions only. Let us go back, then, to the grand significance of a question that is deeply stirring the conscience of the people. And it is indeed expedient today to call the attention of Catholics and of Italians to the main points and to the fundamental characteristics of the compact.

IV

City of the Vatican

The "City of the Vatican" is, first of all, Pontifical territory. It gathers together, shelters within its walls, and exhibits to the veneration of the whole world all the great, significant and precious things that piety, art, science, life and history have offered as an immortal tribute of love and honor to the sacred tomb and the exalted throne of the Prince of the Apostles and to the venerated majesty of his successors. It will be as much territory as the Holy Father judges strictly necessary for his liberty and independence and as acknowledged Father of the Universal Church and as a visible and real sovereign. Let us repeat the word *visible*. It is truly such a sovereignty. A thousand conjectures and long speeches and extensive notices have been broadcast in recent years about the idea of extended territory, though it is indeed smaller than any modern State, and smaller even in proportion to the vastness of jurisdiction of its Sovereign and the number of its subjects.

"We do not claim," this paper declared in 1927, "a guaranty of independence that renders injuries and damages impossible, such as would be the case in an absolute guarantee; such absolute immunity would be impossible in this world. States far more powerful cannot expect this and they have never actually enjoyed it." Yet, no one endowed with common sense would ever suppose that the scarcely discernible borders of Villa Pamfili, or the mere patch of the Sacchetti pinewoods, the bare slopes of a Monte Mario, a square block, a roadway and a group of houses, could be sufficient, we do not say to render the sovereignty of the Pontiff more secure, but simply more visible.

On the other hand this sovereign right, recognized, proclaimed and even codified in the interests of Italy, exercised within or beyond the limits granted by the guarantees . . . however insignificant, because under the control of the Holy Father, becomes at once vested with a power, juridical and moral, that no extent of territory could ever have given it in the matter of efficacy and security.

Here in the little sacred city the civil sovereignty of the Holy Father will be so welded into the religious, his State become so identical with the very principle of his authority, that no violation of it under whatever pretext or political sophistry, it were assumed, could ever be justified or explained in the light of legal equity and culture. To attempt to spoliate this territory would be to cast an insult at the intelligence of the whole world, dishonor the truth of history and stain the hands of justice with sacrilege and such audacity as was perpetrated in Anagni; it would be an act comparable to that which caused the deportation of Pius VI and the capture of Pius VII. Such spoliation would have to be proclaimed under the dark suspicion that the attack was aimed not at self-protection, as was so often pitifully claimed, pretending to save the spiritual, but striking only at the civil right of possession, but it would mean robbing the Pontiff and the Pastor of the Faithful of that least strip of material territory from which the spiritual cannot prescind here on earth. What Leo XIII repeated over and over again in his discourse of October 8, 1883, would then be verified in fact without hope of escape into the deceptive arms of sophistry. "The real purpose of the (Masonic) sects," the Holy Father said, "was to strike at the Church and at its Head."

The consciousness of such hardihood cannot fail to constitute a very natural proof of the inviolability and stability of the treaty: for no territory, however extensive, let us repeat it, and no army, no arsenal (as a mere glance at the political geography of the world will show) could set up any defence against an outrage which will nevertheless have imposed a terrible yoke of insult and suffering that will be to no purpose. This would certainly also be the case if a very well fortified harbor were owned by the Vatican City.

Merely the opening out of property lines is not essential either to the right or to the exercise of sovereignty, even in the event, as has been noted in the press, of the possession of a Papal harbor. We may point out countries like Switzerland, Czechoslovakia, Luxembourg, in Europe, as cases to the point, with San Marino and Andorra; Afghanistan in Asia, Abyssinia in Africa, and Bolivia in America— all of them without outlet to the sea. This strip of land, scarcely discernible in the wide expanse of the Roman Campagna, would look like a characteristic and eloquent example of certain juridic and diplomatic fictions and—of the littleness of human things. For it would be threaded out between lengthy territorial limits, with a precariously narrow diameter to be watched over, so that it would still need more ample protection than all the rest of the Papal State taken together. Even with a hundred-eyed Argus to watch it, it would remain an easy and dangerous breeding ground for disorders, and would be most inconvenient and difficult to be placed under any sort of effective discipline or control.

The financial readjustment that is part of the Italo-Vatican treaty is essential to a valid practico-juridical status. It corresponds, as we have said, to the right that was recognized by the Law of Guarantees itself, which was a recompense to the Holy See for the spoliation of ecclesiastical property and for the old States of the Church that also provided material aid for the increasing spiritual needs of Rome.

It was the Holy Father's duty to make known these needs so that the necessary means of satisfying that right might not be totally denied. By acceding to this request Italy has performed a graceful act of justice and equity.

A capital sum based on the annual apportionment, it will be remembered, had been established in the Law of Guarantees. This sum duly fixed by the Italian State was kindly reduced to a minimum amount by the Holy Father.

V

The Concordat

Throughout these negotiations the treaty was never confused with the Concordat by Pius XI. All pacts and juridical covenants were according to his Holiness' express wish to be enshrined in a spiritual background and their later developments not less than their legal and historical associations were to be ennobled and vitalized by a spiritual significance. For, the spiritual interests of the Italian people must have a very high place in these stipulations and they must be considered as very precious and as an essential element in any process of reconciliation, whether there is question of the stability of the guarantees themselves or the proper regard for the rights and liberty of the Pope. These spiritual interests were to form, as it were, a spiritual fortress about the city of the Vatican more powerful than any walled city or patrolled harbor.

The spirit of fidelity to religion and to the Church coursing in the veins of their forefathers, quickened in the children of a nation in whose bosom Providence placed the See of the Vicar of Christ, will inspire the Italians to safeguard the pontifical interests as their own, and their pledge of full moral sympathy linked by the bond of virtuous living would in due time build up a new vanguard of Christian legions in the beautiful peninsula of the Mediterranean.

"May Italy draw nigh to God," Leo XIII used to repeat to those who saw internal obstacles to an adequate solution of the Roman Question; and "the Lord will provide" was the fervent longing of Pius X. Pius X indeed desired such a boon; Pius XI realizes the long cherished hope.

Once upon a time, none other was needed in order to save a defenseless, humble convent of nuns from the assault of the savage foe than Our Saviour in the Blessed Sacrament, lifted aloft in the pure hands of His poor handmaid, St. Clare. In the same way, enshrined in the heart of the people of Italy He will return to the defense of religious welfare, of education, morals and the entire spiritual life of the nation for present and future generations. This then, will be their treasure and the saving leaven of civic virtues. It is the chief characteristic, the golden seal of that solemn event.

The slur and sneer so often repeated that the Holy Father, covetous of power and dominion had shut himself up in his Petrine prison, "wasting with love of conquest," is void and vanishes forever.

To the peace offered him, to the justice accorded him, to the wealth of benefits that the Church and Christianity will enjoy because of the liberty and independence of their Head,—Pius XI replies by granting his pastoral gift to a reconciled Italy—an unfailing pledge of its most hopeful prosperity.

Dreaming of this happy moment seven years ago the Holy Father had said: "No loftier hymn of praise could have been sung the world over, than that song of the Angels, greeting the humble and peaceful coming of Christ into the world because the Shaper of events and the Author of new mercies was come into our midst."

And that Canticle we too repeat, that it may reëcho in every corner of the globe and in every heart of the heavenly kingdom; in every land and in every soul of the Christian world—"Glory to God in the highest" because He hath given "peace to men of good will."